LIVERPOOL & MANCHESTER

3: Lancashire & Yorkshire Lines

Bob Pixton

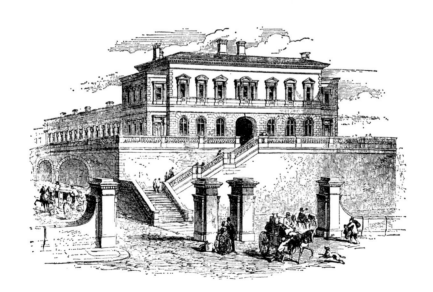

Kestrel Railway Books
PO Box 269
SOUTHAMPTON
SO30 4XR

www.kestrelrailwaybooks.co.uk

Printed by The Amadeus Press

ISBN 978-1-905505-07-4

Front cover: Class 5 4-6-0 No 44803 sets off from Manchester Victoria with the 13.40 to Blackpool (in spite of what the headlamps might suggest!) While this service ran along the original line to Bolton, others using the new direct line transformed the Victorian image of a poor railway company into that of a vibrant, go-ahead enterprise. *(BPC)*

Back cover: Waiting at the Ormskirk bay platform of Rainford Junction on 14th August 1902 is 4-4-0 No 875. Notice the company crest above the driving wheel and the simple initials on the tender. When Barton Wright took over as Chief Mechanical Engineer of the L&Y in 1875, he set about modernising the locomotive fleet. This engine was one of a batch of 20 that the Leeds firm of Kitson built in 1885. Similar to examples from Sharp Stewart, these engines with their 6ft driving wheels did excellent work on express passenger duties. Barton Wright will best be remembered for his standardisation of many features between engines such as boilers, cylinders and driving wheels. Lasting until the winter of 1908, engines of this class were gradually phased out by more powerful engines even though they weren't worn out. *(LCGB, Ken Nunn Collection)*

Liverpool & Manchester

3: Lancashire & Yorkshire Lines

Introduction

Like all the lines between the two cities, this route was opened in several stages and there are, in fact, two routes. The backbone of the original line was the 1838 Manchester, Bolton & Bury Canal Navigation & Railway from Salford. At Bolton, this line met one north to Preston from 1841, and from 1848, the Liverpool & Bury Railway, ending at Great Howard Street, Liverpool. Thus, the L&Y, since that time, had promoted an alternative route from Liverpool to eastern Lancashire and Yorkshire to the LNWR's celebrated line. The small section in Liverpool to Exchange station was opened in 1850, but it would not be until 1865 that the company opened its own lines to Victoria station in Manchester.

The line between the two cities was hardly competitive against other companies like the LNWR and the CLR, as all its trains had to pass via Bolton and Wigan. Indeed, in the mid-1870s, the company was regularly ridiculed in the press for being old, dirty and late. The lack of takeover by the LNWR, the appointment of Barton Wright from Madras Railways and his successor, Aspinall, and the development of Horwich, were to alter this perception. Opening from 1887 to 1889 were a series of new lines and cut-offs that not only transformed services between the two cities, but opened up new territory, and allowed northbound trains to have their first stop at Preston.

These openings put the L&Y into a competitive position, and transformed its outlook and motive power. It soon started to run a competitive service between Liverpool and Manchester, but its celebrated "40 minute express" trains had to be lightly loaded if they were to maintain this very tight schedule over the 36½ mile run. Like the other lines across Lancashire, the L&Y developed a corporate slogan, "The Business Line", from the start of the 20th century. Not only did it transport vast numbers of people to the Lancashire seaside, but it also prided itself on taking businessmen from the coast to the hub of the north west – Manchester. This was continued by the LMS, who ran a publicity campaign, "Make your home in the purer air of Southport", with details of the number of particles in the air for different towns from Salford to the seaside; critics still called the company's operations, "magnified suburban" in character though. Like all larger railways, the company derived the greater part of its revenue from freight, and at Liverpool, tips were built to empty wagons into ships, and trains of 1,000 tons were hauled by specially constructed engines. The original line and the newer "Direct Line" are still open for traffic today.

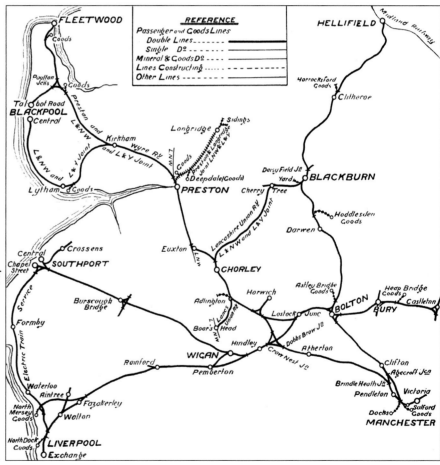

Map of the Line. Not only does this show the original line via Bolton but also the direct line via Atherton and the Wigan avoiding line. These latter two were to play an important part in the revitalisation of the L&Y. Also illustrated are important connections having a bearing on this account, so the line to Preston and the connection to the Midland Railway at Hellifield is shown. The influences of the business from Southport to Liverpool as well as from residential seaside towns such as Southport and Blackpool to Manchester, stand out well.

Tithebarn Street Station, Liverpool.
We are looking at the front of the station with its main 2-storey block, at right angles to which were two single-storey wings (visible in the picture on the title page). Two iron roofs, one of 80ft, the other of 136ft covered the platforms. When it opened on 13th May 1850, there was a single eastern arrival platform and two pairs of departure platforms. The L&Y occupied the western wing and platforms, covered by the larger roof. They wanted to call the station Exchange as it was adjacent to Liverpool's Town Hall, Exchange Square and the Cotton Exchange. The East Lancashire Railway had its facilities in the other half, its platforms covered by the smaller roof; they wanted to call the station Tithebarn Street. The local council displayed a curious attitude to the construction of this station. Some 14 years earlier it had contributed £2,000 towards the construction costs of Lime Street in its attempts to encourage its development in the city centre. When a similar move was made for a station here, there was no such inducement. The station buildings were described as Italianate and hailed (mischievously, I think) as "second in architectural effect to none in Liverpool" in the *Illustrated London News* of 4th May 1850. Due to the presence of the adjacent Leeds & Liverpool Canal, which the line had to cross, the building stood some 30ft above street level, and was reached by an impressive flight of steps. It and the approach arches were completed in 12 months. With ELR and L&Y trains, and later in the year, those of the Liverpool, Crosby & Southport Railway all using one building, it is not surprising that the station was inadequate to cope with the traffic as time went on. *(Liverpool Public Libraries)*

Exchange Station, Liverpool 1989. Due the growth in rail travel in the 1860s and 1870s, the five-platform Tithebarn station became too congested to work properly, so a competition was held for the design of a new station, resulting in a street-level station with ten platforms. Agreement with the Leeds & Liverpool Canal allowed the approaches to be lowered and enlarged to four lines. To ease the congestion, a four track loop was built from the station throat to Exchange Junction, ⅓ mile away, where the lines to Great Howard Street joined the main line. The loop and the western part of the station were opened shortly before

Christmas 1886, and the rest of the high level station was closed for rebuilding, opening in July 1888 with the adjacent hotel a month later. Thus, the L&Y created a compact city centre station for Liverpool, close to the Exchange on Old Hall Street from which it took its name. From the corner of Pall Mall this view down Tithebarn Street shows the clock and the former hotel and station entrances. The stonework has been cleaned for conversion to offices known as "Mercury Court". Although the buildings pre-date the expansion at Manchester's Victoria station by almost 20 years, there are some similarities in the external appearances.
(Tom Wray)

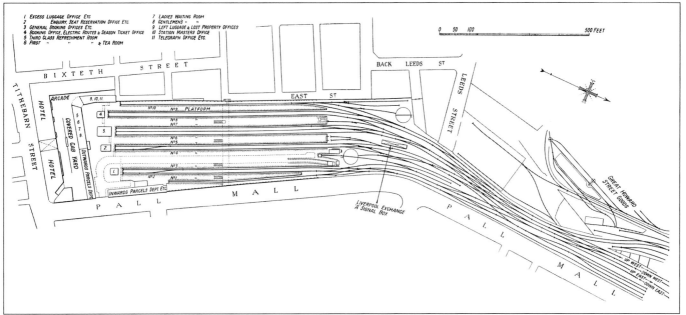

Exchange Station, Liverpool, Track Plan, 1930.
Missing from the plan is the other signalbox ("B" box) that was elevated above the carriage sidings adjacent to Pall Mall. In a few years time the turntable accessible from platform ten would be resited at Bank Hall engine shed (renamed from Sandhills after World War I and a misnomer if ever there was one – there are neither hills nor sand in that location). This operation was possible as the electrification of the lines, not only to Southport, but also to Ormskirk, meant that engines no longer needed to be turned. As can be seen from the plan and subsequent pictures, the station here was adequate and functional, but in no way could it be considered in the grand design of termini – the L&Y at that time did not go in for the Gothic fashion like other companies.

Exchange Station Exterior, 1977. This view is looking north from Tithebarn Street, two weeks before the station closed. It shows the hotel that fronted onto the street and the station entrance, above which was a three faced clock that in L&Y and LMS days (according to legend) was kept fast to ensure passengers were on time! The elegant sandstone facing has been blackened by decades of smoky air; the middle, taller part of the hotel faces down Moorfields, and a bust of John Pearson, Chairman of the Board from 1882, stands there. He was instrumental in leading the transformation of the company, and succeeded in getting the help of John Ramsbottom (of LNWR fame) to assist Barton Wright when he was Locomotive Superintendent. Now, electric trains from Southport, Kirkby and Ormskirk pass along the line from Sandhills, around the site of Great Howard Street depot, and then dive under ground. A new station opened in Moorfields, south of the site of Exchange Station, trains continuing to Liverpool Central and Hunt's Cross.
(JK Williams)

Interior Vehicular Circulating Area, 1977. This view shows the roof over the area set aside for cabs, with an exit onto Pall Mall. Having passed under the hotel (on the right) a traveller would mount a set of steps adjoining the gap in the railings. The foot entrance to the circulating area was through one of the arches on the left, and a tiled map of the L&Y system was high up on the left of the wall. Beyond, was a refreshment room, and around the turn of the century, there would have been segregated areas, not only for the sexes as in toilets, but also for different classes of service. Also accessed from Pall Mall was a separate carriage road for the delivery and collection of mail and parcels, that ran between platforms 3 and 4. *(JK Williams)*

Passenger Circulating Area, 1965. This area appears generous, and was probably photographed at an off-peak time, not that such a term was generally in use (we had "rush hour" then). The terminal lines were in four main groups at the left, with a small building adjacent to the buffer stops. The building in the middle, in front of platforms 6 and 7 was the main booking office. At the end of platforms 4 and 5 was a Midland Railway booking office, which in LMS days, became the place for enquiries and seat reservations. Even at this time, most men were still wearing hats. *(BPC)*

Above left: Exchange Station, 1966. While we might think that barriers and ticket collectors are things of the past, they are making a comeback with automatic barriers. These two platforms were the main departure ones for Southport, although during the rush hour, platform 8 would also be used. In platform 9 is one of the third-generation LMS electric multiple units for the line. The pre-electronic video display describing the train was an interesting innovation, for platforms 7 to 10 (the departure platforms for electric trains) – the names would be illuminated if the train was to stop there. It took until 1960 for loudspeakers to be added to this system of assisting the public. The longitudinal train shed appears adequate for the service here, but it was longer over platforms 1 to 5 (to the right) which were the platforms for main line trains. When the line to Aintree was first electrified, a special shuttle of electric trains ran from here. Then, Grand National day was a Friday, but it changed to a Saturday after World War II. Sandwiched between the two electric motor carriages were ten six-wheelers with a seating capacity of 512 passengers. With ten minutes between trains starting at 11.15am, something like 13,000 people were transported to the course in 1909. An air raid on 3rd May 1940 blew much of the western wall onto the platforms here. *(IG Holt)*

Above right: Exchange Station, 1969. Surely now a collectors item is this company plate at the entrance to the arrivals platform 4. A subway ran underneath the platforms, about half way down their length. This was greatly used for the Aintree race meetings, as passengers could alight from a main line train, and pass along the subway to the platforms where electric trains departed for Aintree (usually platforms 7 to 9) without having to pass through the congested concourse. There were four key busy periods in the station's calendar, when services (especially to Southport) would be stretched. Apart from the race meeting there was Whit Monday, Orangeman's Day (12th July) and August Bank Holiday. In 1928, the station staff numbered around 280 people. To accommodate the wave of emigration from Northern Europe and Scandinavia, special trains carried passengers from Hull across England to Liverpool. At Great Howard Street there were "extensive barrack waiting rooms" for the trans-Atlantic ship passengers. *(A Sommerfield)*

Exchange Station, 1915. For World War I, the L&Y built a special ambulance train of 16 bogie coaches that toured important towns in 1915 before going to the Continent. So long was the train, that when it was displayed in Manchester's Victoria station on 31st January and 1st February 1915, it occupied both platforms 9 and 10. The display was opened to the public here by the Lord Mayor, with around £300 being raised and donated, "to the provision of comforts for the wounded in hospital in Liverpool District". To control the crowds, the company would have used its own police force, which numbered about 100 officers and detectives, and had an office here with the

HQ at Victoria. Its main role wasn't catching criminals, but crime prevention by making effective patrols, padlocking vans and securing the perimeter goods yards, as petty theft from unsecured wagons was a source of loss. Here, the train describer consists of station names on slats of wood that could be rotated to give different destinations. Over platform 5 there is a special notice for the fast service to Manchester. The flat pieces suspended from the roof are smoke deflectors that protected the roof from engines' exhausts. *(BPC)*

Exchange Station, c1894. Arriving on the down fast line, and signalled to go into either platform 1, 2 or 3, is an Aspinall 4-4-0 engine with its 7ft 3in driving wheels. This type of engine was a development of the Beyer Peacock engines with a similar wheel arrangement but 6ft driving wheels. They would be expected to handle the express passenger work, and given that the 40-minute trains between the cities were only three or four coaches, they were able to do this job well; the Atlantic engines were a logical development of this type of engine from 1899. There were originally two turntables, this one (between the approaches to platforms 3 and 4) was 50ft long, and lasted until the end of steam. There was space for a turntable, as a carriage road was built between the platforms. *(BPC)*

Exchange Station, 1965. In charge of the 3.00pm to Rochdale, is Stanier 2-6-4T No 42647 on 27th June, waiting at platform 4. It would stop at all stations, except Kirkdale, via Wigan, Bolton and Bury, arriving at 5.09pm. While the speed was slow (a little over 20mph) the connections afforded were great, notwithstanding a wait of 24 minutes at Bolton. Long wheelbase tank locomotives like this were ideal for suburban passenger services: this one was built at Derby in 1938/9. Note that by this time, the cab road was being used as a source of income – car parking. *(HC Casserley)*

Exchange Station, June 1954. Preparing to leave platform 6 with the 8.30am to Yorkshire is "Black 5" 4-6-0 No 44690 pulling its "blood & custard" coaches. (This engine was one of the last batch of 40 built in 1950 at Crewe, and lasted right up to the end of steam.) The actual cost of the engine and tender had doubled since their pre-war price of £6,500. After separation at Halifax, Leeds (Central) would be reached at 11.03 and Bradford (Exchange) at 10.56. This service was approximately hourly from 9.30am to 4.30pm. Before the "Direct Line" was built, the congestion at Manchester Victoria station caused problems for such trains. An ingenious solution was found whereby the train was made up of two parts at Liverpool Exchange, one for Manchester and the other for Rochdale and Yorkshire. Both portions would travel via Wigan to Bolton, where they would separate, the Yorkshire section avoiding Manchester completely going via Bury and Rochdale, and the remaining part going to Salford and Victoria. The different lengths of the roofs show up here, the longer one over platforms 1 to 5 extending on the left. A flight of steps led down to the subway that went under the platforms. *(BPC)*

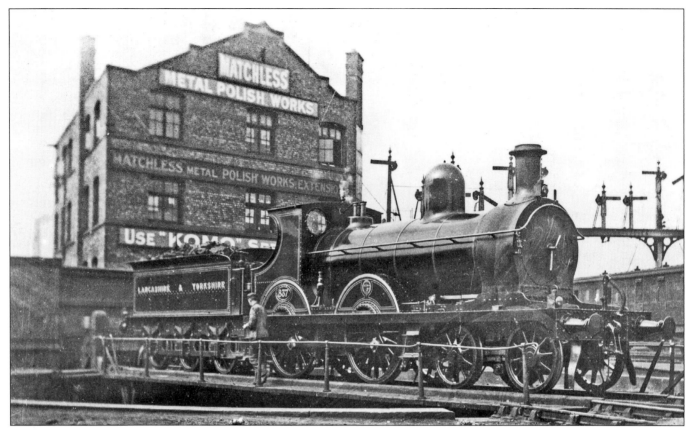

Exchange Station, 1902. This part of the approach to the station is built over Leeds Street at the start of the canal to that city. One of the factories on that street made "Matchless" metal polish. Of the two original turntables, this one serving the western side (the higher-numbered platforms) was less used after electrification from 1904. Resplendent in the August sun is 4-4-0 No 837, but sadly it would only see service until September of the following year, being only 19 years old when withdrawn. It was painted black with the narrow lines being white, and any broad lines painted red. The company's name was shaded, and on the splasher was the company crest. To arrive at Tithebarn Street, the railway had to cross above the canal at the insistence of the canal company, necessitating the height of the station compared to the surroundings. Later, the canal company relented and allowed the canal arms to be blocked, to allow a lower level building. *(LCGB, Ken Nunn Collection)*

Exchange Station, 1954. Having just left platform 5 is BR Clan class 4-6-0 No 72001 *Clan Cameron*, probably bound for Scotland. From 1876, with the opening of the line to Hellifield and the Settle-Carlisle main line, the Midland Railway started to

operate trains to Scotland. At Blackburn, through coaches from Liverpool joined those from Manchester Victoria to Edinburgh and Glasgow. Soon, this train will cross over to the fast lines towards Walton Junction. Ahead is 136-lever signalbox No1 (or 'B' cabin), astride a carriage siding, which was eventually replaced by a smaller flat-roofed cabin on the opposite side of the line. Colour lights replaced semaphores in 1937. A bridge takes the railway across the LNWR line to Waterloo goods station, on the left. *(JA Peden)*

Exchange Station, 1963. Leaving platform 6 is a train bound for Glasgow, hauled by Jubilee class No 45719 *Glorious* with a class 5 4-6-0 as pilot. The route it has been given is the up slow, which it will take through Sandhills and Kirkdale stations to Walton Junction, where it will take the former East Lancashire Railway to Preston to meet the West Coast Main Line and the through carriages for Glasgow and Edinburgh from Manchester. The line was subject to low (30-35mph) speed limits, so "slow" was an appropriate designation. The train is just about to go behind signal cabin "A" (or No 2) with its 169 levers, built in 1887. *(BPC)*

Exchange Station, 1939. What a splendid quartet of engines! On the extreme left is a 2-6-4T at platform 1, probably with a local service. A pair of class 5 4-6-0 engines flank the next pair of platforms with No 5217 at platform 2 and sister engine 5206 at platform 3, and an unidentifiable similar engine graces platform 4, all proudly proclaiming their company ownership. While in L&Y days the non-stop expresses to Manchester normally took 40 minutes, in LMS days a standard time of 45 minutes was adopted for this and the LNWR line. In 1886, there were 216 trains in and out of the station, rising to over 300 by 1928. There is not a spot of litter, and the roof is intact. *(ER Morten)*

Exchange Station, 1902. On the turntable is 6-year old "Radial" 2-4-2T No 76. All railway companies needed engines to pull their stopping trains with a fair turn of speed, and 5ft 8in driving wheels were used here, often with good performances on some express trains as well. Some companies used a different wheel arrangement (for example, 0-4-4T) but Aspinall reasoned that this version was more balanced, so would give smoother running. The sort of duties they would have performed were stopping trains to Wigan, and probably also to Bolton and Rochdale. In pre-electrification days, they also hauled Southport and Ormskirk services. Later that year, it would become standard to display the words of the company in a bold arc over the number plate. These locomotives had vacuum operated water scoops that could be used in both directions, and a new Belpaire boiler in 1915 would take this engine (renumbered 10728 by the LMS) up to August 1948, when it was withdrawn. *(LCGB, Ken Nunn Collection)*

Exchange Station, c1950. Looking towards the buffer stops along platform 3 this picture illustrates the wide cab road between it and platform 4 on the right; some of the abundant hand trolleys are laden ones servicing the train there. Note the railings around the steps down to the subway, the roof support pillars actually partially block them on platform 2 – a pattern repeated on

platforms 5/6 and 7/8. The other side of the brick wall on the left is Pall Mall, and inside is the shorter platform 1 with Aspinall 2-4-2T No 50721 of 1895 vintage. Jobs would include removing coaches from arriving trains to allow the engines to be serviced. The main carriage sidings were either side of the line at Kirkdale, although there was limited accommodation by signalbox No 1. Coaches might also have to be diagrammed to be used on another service, and would have to be moved to that platform. Often pilot engines would fit in short timetabled trains as well, for example to Preston or Wigan. *(HC Casserley)*

Exchange Station, 1965. Looking neglected is Jubilee class 4-6-0 No 45721 *Impregnable*. The Exchange station was probably the principle station for residents to travel from when visiting the seaside, either at Southport (by electric train), Blackpool (by trains such as this, the 12.27pm) or Morecambe. On the left is the L&Y water column at the end of platforms 1 and 2. Not long after being photographed, this engine was withdrawn after giving 29 years

service. The original Stanier tender ordered for it in 1936 was allocated to one of the Royal Scot class, this engine getting the smaller Fowler tender from engine No 6100. In 1939/40 a similar manoeuvre was done with larger 4,000 gallon tenders intended for class 4F 0-6-0s. However, when some Patriot class engines were rebuilt in 1946/9, their smaller tenders were swapped for some Jubilee ones... *deja vu*! Eventually, in 1958/64, one from a Stanier 8F was attached. *(IG Holt)*

No 1 Signalbox, 1971. Due to the continual removal of levers, the original box started to list, so in 1963 it was knocked down and replaced on the other side of the line in the lifted trackbed. In true BR fashion, it had a flat roof, and was of all-timber construction – the hallmarks of a cheap, temporary job. It closed in 1977. *(MA King)*

Great Howard Street, 1954. This was the site of the original passenger terminus in the city for the line from Manchester, from 1849 to 1850. Two of the obstacles to the original joint (L&Y and ELR) plan to enter the city centre resulted in a temporary terminus here. One of these obstacles was the east to west line of the LNWR on its way to Waterloo goods station (overcome by the erection of a bridge), but the other (the Leeds & Liverpool Canal) was a different matter. It must be remembered that the 127¼ mile canal was Britain's

most successful long distance canal from its opening in 1742, and as they wouldn't close the relevant parts, the railway had to go over the top. When Tithebarn Street opened, this became a goods depot for the rest of its existence, until the late 1960s. The track in the middle of the picture descends to service the street level goods warehouse, while those to the right serve the top levels of the warehouse. On the left is the elevated No 1 signalbox, with coaches on the approach lines to Exchange station. *(Railway & Canal Historical Society)*

Great Howard Street, 1960. As in Manchester, the space beneath the approach arches was valuable to the L&Y. However, their utilisation depended on there being adequate access. Here, as at Salford, lines led down a steep gradient, but engines such as "Pug" 0-4-0ST No 51227 had limited braking power as they only weighed just over 21 tons. Consequently, they could only cope with short trains if they weren't to be dragged down uncontrollably, but bigger engines wouldn't have been able to negotiate the sharp curves evident here. When the station approaches were being built, the L&Y board discussed the arches in 1885, and accepted the financial argument that rental of £432 10s per annum was a better return than the capital cost of £6,224 to fill them in. *(JK Williams)*

Great Howard Street, 1913. This view, from an adjacent tall building, shows the greatly expanded outdoor part of the goods depot. Chaotic as it seems, there was an orderliness about it, and as they were in existence for so long, such places must have worked to an extent. People were employed to do specific jobs including chasing up missing loads. Across the back is the viaduct and girder approach with Exchange station on the right. Signalbox

'B' with its 136 levers is raised up for better viewing in a restricted site and has a carriage siding under it. Behind the large building in the centre, the main lines divide to give greater track capacity, and the main lines cross the LNWR lines to Waterloo goods depot by the girder bridge to the right of the water tank. In front of the water tank, tracks lead down to the goods yard. *(BPC)*

Great Howard Street, 1914. The goods depot here was mostly for businesses in the city centre with deliveries by van. However, that wasn't always the case, and before World War II, most journeys would have been made by horse and cart. This is entrance No 3 to the L&Y goods shed, with a company dray posing for the photograph. In 1945, there were some 60 horses attached here, stabled under the arches of the line from Exchange near Love Lane. This complement was made up of about twelve Suffolk Punches, an equal number of Clydesdales, and the remainder crossbreeds. The average weight of such an animal would be around a ton. (The 1948 equine flu outbreak meant that deliveries were delayed during the six-week period.) By 1954, all deliveries by live horses had been replaced by Scammell "mechanical horse" 3-wheel tractors with trailers. *(BPC)*

Pier Head, Liverpool, 1954.
The large goods stations of the L&Y were concentrated to the north of the city and in Bootle. However, they did have modest incursions to the south. These were at South Docks, sandwiched between the LNWR and Cheshire Lines Brunswick warehouses on Sefton Street, and from 1902, an additional depot on the corner of Wapping and Salthouse Lane, adjacent to the imposing Custom House landmark building. The company also had a "City Office & Receiving Depot" in Victoria Street, which closed in December 1914 after the enlargement to the Wapping & Salthouse Lane

depot. There was no connection between these depots and the rest of the L&Y empire, except via the Mersey Docks & Harbour Board lines. Here, "Pug" 0-4-0ST No 51206 (at least sixty years old) is bringing traffic to a standstill; note the sheeted wagons to protect the goods from the elements. Wooden blocks at the front and rear of the engine prevented the buffers of the engine and wagon becoming locked when shunting around sharp curves, which was their niche in life. Originally, trains were restricted to 12 wagons at a walking pace preceded by a man with a red flag or lamp – the length of the train might have increased with business over time, but the mechanism for its progress remained distinctly Victorian. The now goods-only dock lines at this point passed underneath those of the passenger-only Liverpool Overhead Railway. *(BPC)*

Opposite page: Exchange Station Junction. When the station was rebuilt in the 1880s, it was decided to increase the number of approach roads. This was achieved by putting four tracks on a viaduct slightly to the east of the lines to Great Howard Street. During the Blitz of 7/8th May 1941, the signalbox was destroyed, and its replacement was an LMS flat-topped cabin housing 60 levers that lasted until 1969. The breach of the viaduct here caused Wigan services to terminate at Preston Road initially, but later at Kirkdale. Those from Preston terminated at Aintree, and electric trains ran to Kirkdale, with buses making connections to the city centre. Normal services to Exchange did not resume until 2nd May 1942, and in fact, passengers destined for Manchester were encouraged to travel from Central or Lime Street stations. To co-ordinate clearance work, the LMS set up a committee that met frequently until the end of May at the Adelphi Hotel in Liverpool. One report they had to deal with was that on 8th May the port was virtually at a standstill. On the human scale they had to contend with 12,000 people rendered homeless, so they ran special trains to Upholland and Wigan to evacuate them and workman's trains to and from the city for the next few days. The lower picture shows the new viaduct being built, with the columns and concrete springings for the arches in place. *(Both BRB Residuary Ltd)*

L&Y Ships. *Mellifont* was originally built for the Liverpool to Drogheda service, which left from Princess Landing Stage – not the best arrangement as Exchange station was some distance away, but considering the LNWR route was to Lime Street station, it was comparable. The service to Ireland was twice weekly from 1902 until the outbreak of World War I. With the company's services to Goole in the east, a passenger could travel from Ireland to the Continent completely by Lancashire & Yorkshire Railway – a marketing slogan that the railway used. *(BR)*

Sandhills, 1966 (above) 1968 (right). A mile and a half north of the terminus is this station built over (and accessed from) Sandhills Lane. On the eastern side of the station is the Huskisson goods station of the Cheshire Lines, and to the west is that company's Victoria yard, with the Midland Railway Canada & Sandon goods station beyond that; a short covered way under the southern end of the station links these yards. Originally there were just two L&Y lines, but they were quadrupled for the expansion of the new terminus at Exchange. The whole station was of timber construction with concrete supports and paving slabs for platform edges in some places; covered steps led down to a booking office. The view from the cab of an engine is along the up fast line, the fine signal gantry ahead indicating that the driver is to continue along that route at the crossover at the end of the platform. Passengers on the island platform are resting against a screen to give them some protection from the wind as the station is on an embankment. From the down slow platform, trains have a choice of routes – Southport or Kirkdale. *(Lancashire & Yorkshire Railway Society, HF Wheller)*

Above: Sandhills, c1960s. Having left Exchange station some four minutes ago, the driver of class 5 4-6-0 No 44882 will be keen to pick up speed as the first stop is not likely to be until Wigan or Preston. Apart from speed restrictions along the way (as at Walton Junction) good speeds for the day were maintained to keep to the timetable. The way the platforms are constructed is illustrated well, as is the means by which passengers were protected from strong winds. *(Brian Taylor)*

Left: Sandhills Station, 1961. Racing through on the up fast is BR Standard 2-6-0 No 78041 on 4th May, which will take the coaches to Preston from where they will continue to Glasgow. Little was spent on passenger facilities on this, the platform for the down fast line, as few trains stopped here. The island platform has concrete supports with slabs on top, and is the only one open at the 1974 station. A train on the up slow line would have a choice of routes, as indicated by the fine bracket signal. On the extreme right are the lines to the docks and coal tips with tank No 47231 and a train of coal wagons. *(BPC)*

Sandhills, 1924. It is only a year after the Grouping, and the scene here at the north end of the station remains true to its parent company, with lots of lower quadrant signals. On the left is a train hauled by an unidentified 0-8-0 towards the High Level tips along the "coal lines". By means of this branch, coal could be tipped directly into waiting vessels at Wellington and Bramley Moore docks. *(Milepost 92½ Picture Library, AWV Mace Collection)*

Clarence Dock, 1962. In 1929, Clarence Dock closed and a coal-fired power station was built on the site. Wagons would have to traverse the MD&HB lines to the power station. Hunslet 0-6-0ST No 9 hauls a train of empty hopper wagons from the power station. Purchased new in 1940, this engine would last until 1962. *(The Transport Treasury, Alec Swain)*

Sandhills, 1968. This picture was taken from inside a DMU on the up fast line on its way north from Liverpool. Stanley Road bridge is ahead, and the signalbox on the right is Sandhills No1 with its 145 levers, which replaced two boxes in the 1937 resignalling scheme. This was a very complex area with important junctions and crossovers. On the left, behind the photographer, the four lines from North Docks Goods and the High Level Coal Branch met the four lines from Exchange Station. In front, four lines go straight on to Kirkdale flanked by goods lines, and six lines curve west to Bank Hall and Southport. The movement between up, down, fast and slow for both routes must have presented particular problems for signalling staff. This train has been given the "Wigan up slow" route by the signals in front. *(HF Wheller)*

Bank Hall station, 1966. While the lines to Wigan curve away to the east, those to Southport curve north. The four passenger lines are well illustrated, with a down train leaving the station and passing under Bankhall Street bridge. Ahead of it are Sandhills and Exchange stations. On the left is part of the extensive sidings in the area serving the canal coal tips. A typical L&Y two-colour brick booking office sits astride the two island platforms with steps going down to them. With trams encroaching on their business, coupled with Exchange working close to capacity, the decision was made to electrify this line to Southport in 1902. With almost a doubling of the number of trains, and a reduction in journey time by a third, the system is still going strong over 100 years later. *(IG Holt)*

Bank Hall, 1955. In charge of the 9.40am to Leeds on 23rd August is class 5 4-6-0 No 44692. The route would be via Manchester Victoria (10.28) and Summit tunnel, arriving at Bradford Exchange (12.03) or Leeds (12.12), after the train had been divided at Low Moor. This engine was one of 40 built in 1947, and had a life of only 16 years. It is travelling along the fast lines, and has just gone under Stanley Road. The photographer was standing over the entrance line to Bank Hall locomotive depot. On the left is the bridge over the Cheshire Lines route to Huskisson, built so that quadrupling at a later date could easily be accommodated; far sighted planning indeed. *(Brian Morrison)*

Bank Hall Locomotive Depot, 1957. This was built adjacent to the L&Y main line just beyond where the line to Southport departed north on the other side of the Stanley Road bridge from where this picture was taken. The shed visible is half of the 1860s building. Originally there were eight roads, all leading to a turntable at the back of the site, and to the rear of the loco shed, deep in a cutting, was the LNWR Bootle branch, making the site very cramped. By the mid-1870s, the shed was too small to deal with all the engines from Exchange station and some of the nearby docks, and that was after the opening of Aintree Shed in 1866. The new 8-road shed was to the east of the old one, and was accessed by the two lines beyond Sandhills No 2 signalbox; all the engines shared the servicing facilities. In the 1930s, the area was modernised, changing its name from Sandhills just after World War I. During that war, the redundant turntable from Exchange replaced the original one here (the

electrification of the Southport line reducing the need for it). To improve facilities, half the old shed was demolished, and an ash plant and concrete coaling stage were built in a "cafeteria" layout. Two tank engines (a Kitson 0-4-0ST and 51229) are dwarfed by the structures. 0-6-0T No 47230 is waiting on the up west goods line, the ground signals by the side of it being operated by some of the 76 levers in the adjacent signalbox. Kirkdale carriage sidings are in the background, with the electrified pair of lines passing to Kirkdale in the distance. The "Wigan" or fast pair of lines are to the right. The shed prided itself on having the smartest breakdown train in the country, and an engine in steam was always kept attached to the crane and vans. *(JA Peden)*

Bank Hall, 1937. This glorious view of shed No 23A in the LMS system was taken from the top of the coaling tower. On the right is the roof of the original shed with the newer 8-road shed in full view. The LNWR Bootle branch Atlantic Dock Junction is between the shed and the row of houses in the background, some 50 feet below. A forgotten facet of steam train operation is the rate at which it demanded coal, and in 1955, it is estimated that over 12 million tons of coal were used for locomotives alone. For six days after the May blitz in 1941, the depot was without water, which must have caused many difficulties for servicing engines. *(BPC)*

Rear of Bank Hall Locomotive Depot, 1930. Expansion of the locomotive depot was restricted due to the LNWR Bootle branch. This wonderful picture is of a short cutting between two tunnels. In front is a tunnel under the L&Y line at Kirkdale that leads to Edge Hill. This line is to Canada Dock, while the branch on the left, behind the18-lever Atlantic Dock Junction signalbox, is for connections to Southport at Bootle Junction along the L&Y, and Alexandra Dock. Argos Road is to the left, and up above the wall on the right is Bank Hall locomotive depot. *(D Ibbotson)*

Bank Hall, c1924. With The Melrose public house making up the background, this picture nicely shows a "before and after" view of Hughes 4-6-0 engines at L&Y shed No18. On the right is No 1512 dating from 1908, whose home shed was No 17, Southport. One of the duties for this engine was a trip from home to Manchester and back with a run here in-between. The engine was one of the few not rebuilt and was worn out two years later, hence it never carrying the number allocated to it by the LMS, 10402. The other engine, No 10431, was only two years old, and benefited from being built with Walschaerts valve gear and superheating; it would last another 12 years. By the end of the L&Y, around 40% of the engines allocated here were for passenger turns. Most of these were 2-4-2T locomotives, followed by 4-4-0s. There were five Hughes 4-6-0s, with six 4-4-2s sharing the crack express trains. As a rule of thumb, the company had eight engines sidelined for repairs or maintenance for every ten hauling trains; today's margins would be much lower, as engines are more reliable and expected to do more to earn their keep. *(L&GRP)*

Bank Hall, 1946. Aspinall introduced these class 24 0-6-0T "Rapid Shunters" in 1897, ordering 20 engines from the company's Horwich works. With their small, 4ft diameter wheels and short wheelbase they were a compromise between power and an ability to go anywhere – somewhere between a "Pug" and a Barton Wright saddle tank. Starting as L&Y No 1355, it became the LMS number shown here before being allocated its BR number, 51535, in 1950 for the last six years of its life. The smoke deflector (see opposite) has been swivelled to the open position, and we can see some interesting buffers. Because of a tendency to dart forward, these engines were not popular with train crews, especially the one that almost demolished Brindle Heath Junction signalbox in 1910! *(HC Casserley)*

Bank Hall, 1932. No account of the shed would be complete without a picture of the famous "High-Flyer" class, here with LMS No 10310, and ready for duty. This "Ten wheeler" was one of the first series, being built at Horwich in June 1899 as No 1402. It more than lived up to Aspinall's expectations, as it had a life of 34 years, four more than he thought was a reasonable life span for an engine. Although beaten by a year by Ivatt of the Great Northern Railway to introduce such Atlantic engines, the reaction from the railway press came out in favour of Aspinall's engines. *Locomotive Magazine* remarked that the GNR engines were "new and interesting" and "possessing many points of more than ordinary merit". However, it called the L&Y engines "very remarkable express locomotives" and "unique". While this engine's boiler was only a few inches longer and bigger than its rivals, the commentator described it as "eclipsing anything hitherto attempted in this country." Aspinall and Ivatt had been friends since their younger days at Crewe and later as colleagues in Ireland, so their reaction to these comments would have been interesting to hear. *(W Stubbs)*

"Pugs", Cheek-to-Cheek, 1946. To cope with the sharp bends in the docks, the L&Y bought and then copied a Vulcan short wheelbase 0-4-0ST. So that the buffers of the engine and the wagons didn't become locked together on the tight curves, the engines had blocks of wood instead of buffers. Both examples were built in 1906, and survived well into the BR period. They were fitted with a smoke deflector which could be either rotated over the chimney or away from it in an "open" position. These were fitted at the request of the Liverpool Overhead Railway, to reduce corrosion of their Barlow decking. Neither engine has the metal cab-side shutters that other residents of this depot had. Respectively they carried the numbers 51231 and 51232, with the left-hand engine covering over half a million miles before they were both withdrawn in 1963. *(HC Casserley)*

Kirkdale Tunnels. As most railways experienced in Liverpool, there is a ridge of sandstone rock around the central area. The original Liverpool & Manchester railway had a deep cutting at Olive Mount, east of their Edge Hill station, and to overcome the barrier to progress into central Liverpool, they built a series of tunnels leading to the terminal station at Lime Street. At first, the Cheshire Lines terminated at Brunswick until they too built a tunnel approach to their Liverpool Central station. Only the line from Sandhills to Southport did not have a tunnel or deep cutting because it hugged the coast. The main L&Y line east passed under the Breeze Hill area of Bootle, which was mentioned in the Domesday Book. Later, the area was described as somewhere where the people were "considered respectable", and a covered reservoir was built on top of the rock. As planned jointly by the East Lancashire and the Liverpool & Bury Railways, there was a single tunnel of 1,149yd with up and down lines in it. Later on it became a serious obstacle to services from Wigan and Preston to Liverpool. However, it wasn't until 1901 that plans were made for its enlargement, and land bought for the disposal of the spoil. The plans involved making the existing tunnel shorter, with gap of 111yd in the middle to create two shorter tunnels, and building a new pair of lines to the west in tunnels to match. Just before the shorter tunnel of 210 yards, there was a footbridge from which the picture above was taken.

Above: No 2 Tunnel. Looking north at the southern tunnel we see the signals for Walton Junction in the up direction and the back of the signal gantry for Kirkdale East in the down direction. It shows that it was possible to transfer from fast to slow, and also from slow to fast lines. The latter option was later removed at this location. South of Walton Junction, there were effectively two separate pairs of lines.

Opposite page, top: No1 Tunnel. This is the southern portal of the longer, 498yd, northern tunnel. When the new pair of lines was ready in 1903, traffic moved over to them so that work could progress on the old tunnel, all four lines opening the next year. This involved taking down the stonework at the portals, numbering the pieces and then, rebuilding them at the ends of the shorter tunnel's mouths. However, some of the marks had become obliterated during the time they were stacked, and a massive jigsaw puzzle was the result. The western pair was electrified in 1906 as far as Aintree, and eventually, Ormskirk, the line continuing to Preston. The eastern pair was "steam only" to Wigan. Trains not stopping at the inner suburban stations tended to use the Wigan lines, so they became designated "fast lines", this arrangement existing all the way from Exchange station, some 2½ miles to the south west. The walls are littered with refuges for workers on the line to hide in when trains pass. Very hazardous! *(Both D Ibbotson)*

Walton Junction, 1960. Looking west on 30th May from the footbridge, this picture sees Fairburn 2-6-4T No 42297 with a train for Manchester Victoria. The signalbox to the rear of the train is Walton Junction, a 1903 replacement with 60 levers. To the right is the former Liverpool, Ormskirk & Preston Railway, later absorbed by the East Lancashire Railway. Opening a year after the Wigan line, they operated as two separate railways before uneasily amalgamating under the L&Y banner 10 years later in 1859. After the junction, the lines were organised into slow (north) and fast (south) with connections between the Preston and Wigan lines as the signals indicate. An early indication of things to come arrived early in World War II, when on 18th September 1940, bomb damage blocked all the lines here. While the slow lines were cleared almost immediately by the next evening, the Wigan lines were cut resulting in diversion of traffic until the damage could be repaired. *(BPC)*

Walton Junction Station, c1900. In an area famous for its prison, a third line would soon be added for the electric trains that went as far as Aintree (1906), Maghull (1909), Town Green (1911) and finally Ormskirk (1913). It was hoped that this mode of transport could achieve several ends, one being to avoid the problems of steam train operation (smoke, dirt and the cost of the fuel). However, at that time there was reluctance to use capital for a project that would be overtaken by advances in technology a few years later. Therefore, even though the Board was apprehensive, it was the vision of the General Manager, Aspinall that won the day. *(Lens of Sutton Collection)*

Preston Road, 1961.
Emerging from under the bridge on 4th May is class 5 4-6-0 No 44887. As the line has now been operated by EMUs for over 30 years, it is perhaps hard for us to realise the importance of this route in pre-motorway days. Not only were there express trains for Manchester, Leeds, Newcastle, Blackpool and York, but also local services to Rainford Junction and Wigan, with many trains to Bolton, Bury and Rochdale as well. This one is destined for Hull, and would have been expected to travel to Wigan in 27 minutes some 45 years ago. *(Frank Dean)*

Preston Road, c1919. This was where the line to Wigan went under the main road to Preston. The line to Preston was a stone's throw away, but the station on that line was called Walton Junction. To avoid confusion from 1984, this one was renamed Rice Lane. Stone steps led down from the road, with both platforms having some facilities. On the Wigan side was a wooden structure, while the brick building on the Liverpool side contained the booking office. Before it was replaced, the roof overhung the building, and obscured the standard L&Y clock; the gas lamps had the station's name on them. The signals for Walton Junction, just round the bend under the distant footbridge, are on a gantry as there was a possibility at that time for exchanges between both fast and slow lines. The goods yard boasted a 6-ton crane. *(John Ryan Collection)*

Hartley's Sidings.

Approximately ¾ mile north of Preston Road station, the jam maker's factory was on the down side of the line (seen here with wagons on it) and accessed by a trailing slip. Hartley's Siding was the next box from Walton Junction, where the line went under the Cheshire Lines, to which Hartleys also had a connection (bottom of picture). The factory was adjacent to Long Lane with access from Hartley Avenue. Above the entrance was the owner's name, William Pickles Hartley. The factory opened in 1886, eventually covering 10 acres and producing 600 tons of jam a week. Many shops bought 7lb jars of jam and sold portions of it to customers. *(John Ryan Collection)*

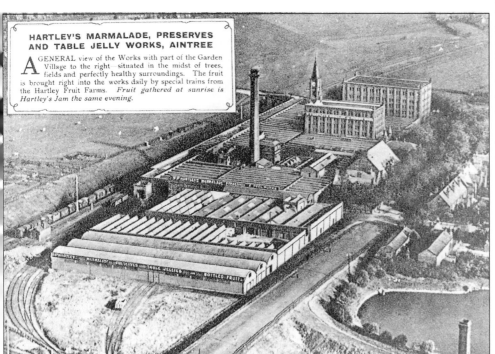

HARTLEY'S MARMALADE, PRESERVES AND TABLE JELLY WORKS, AINTREE

A GENERAL view of the Works with part of the Garden Village to the right—situated in the midst of trees, fields and perfectly healthy surroundings. The fruit is brought right into the works daily by special trains from the Hartley Fruit Farms. *Fruit gathered at sunrise is Hartley's Jam the same evening.*

Fazakerley, 1959. From its opening in 1848, the station here has been variously called Simonswood and Aintree, but it wasn't until after the L&Y absorbed the East Lancashire Railway in 1859, that it settled on Fazakerley. This view is from the Liverpool platform with its greater facilities and a fine metal footbridge joining it to the other. A small, 20-lever signalbox was behind the photographer, controlling a level crossing there as well. Racing through the passenger-only station on its way east is unusual visitor, unnamed Patriot 4-6-0 No 45517 on 22nd September. *(BPC)*

Fazakerley, 1966. Looking north east, this view shows the station buildings on the platform for Liverpool, and as lesser patronage was expected for journeys to Wigan a wooden shelter was thought sufficient, but even Liverpool-bound passengers didn't have a canopy. On the left is the bracket signal, indicating the start of an up loop, obscured from us by the footbridge but lifted high to aid visibility to drivers. From this loop, access to the company's wagon repair workshops could be gained. In the distance is the small (20 levers) signalbox that controlled the up and down goods loops, as well as the main line. Adjacent, was a footpath crossing the line to Signal Works Road, where the Railway Signal Co had its premises. About a half a mile along the line, the line from Exchange station met the line west from North Mersey at Fazakerley Junction.
(Lancashire & Yorkshire Railway Society)

Fazakerley Sidings, 1957. Looking towards the junction from Sidings West signalbox this shows a trainload of coal destined for the docks. Austerity class 2-8-0 No 90599 is signalled to proceed along the down main line, its destination likely to be Aintree sorting sidings, about a mile ahead. On the left are the extensive sidings where trains were broken and re-assembled. A nightmare for those trying to manage the situation is a report by the General Manager to the Board of the L&Y on 9th May 1906. He reported that Aintree sidings were blocked, and this galvanised the Board into action, authorising £4,500 to be spent on additional sidings to be built there, which opened in 1911. In that year, three out of every five freight trains carried

coal, and while ordinary goods earned the company more money per ton carried, it was the sheer volume of coal that dictated the number of trains, hence the development of traffic control offices here, at Wigan and at Victoria station in Manchester from 1912. In that year over 3.6 million tons was moved by the L&Y. Developments in technology made telephones more reliable, allowing better communications between control offices and goods depots. The Railway Signal Company had premises on the right, accessed from the main line. This company was responsible for the signalling arrangements at Liverpool Exchange Station when it was completed in 1888. *(JA Peden)*

Fazakerley Sidings, 1911. The vast amount of coal is difficult for us to comprehend without pictures like this. Built in 1889, there was capacity for 1,860 wagons, but this was dwarfed by nearby Aintree's 3,126 wagon capacity. Coal production had climbed from 128 million tons in 1870 to 181 million tons 20 years later, and 10 years after that it became 225 million tons. Two years after this picture was taken, the peak was reached at 287 million tons. While much of this was for the home market, in that year 73 million tons was exported, and much was used to bunker ships, especially at Liverpool. From the turn of the century, the origins of the coal arriving here altered. With the exhaustion of much of the south Lancashire coalfield, more coal now came from Yorkshire, and this is mirrored by the age of the wagons on show. The older wagons have BB on them, indicating Blundells colliery near Wigan, while the Henry Lodge wagons were from Yorkshire, and were much newer. *(NRM)*

Traffic Control Office, Aintree. An office opened here in June 1912 close to the sorting sidings. However, when the Central Control Office opened in Manchester in August 1915, this office still continued to operate. The area under control was to Southport, Burscough Junction, Fazakerley and Rainford Junction. Following bombing in May 1941, it was temporarily located by Aintree station, but in post-war years it was located at the west end of the gridiron, lasting (like the sidings) until around 1964. The building survived in various guises for many years, ultimately being demolished to make way for a new car showroom. *(BPC)*

Aintree Racecourse Station, 1912. The main passenger route for trains from the east was south at Fazakerley Junction for Liverpool's Exchange station. However, at the important Spring Meeting at Aintree racecourse (which includes The Grand National) some of the special passenger trains went along the line towards North Mersey to access the station adjacent to the racecourse. The station was unique in that the up line was lifted slightly, and the area covered in compacted fine cinders, including the up line, up to an informal platform edge. Passengers are seen leaving the coaches, passing across the cinder platform and the up line, and going straight into the racecourse. In 1934, the LMS ran 22 special trains here, and in 1958, there were 14. Starting life about 1890 as Aintree Cinder Lane, the station changed its name in 1910. *(NRM)*

Aintree, Sefton Arms, 1956. This was on the line from Walton Junction to Preston (electrified as far as Ormskirk). LMS 2P 4-4-0 No 40581, with an unidentified 4-6-0, is at the excursion platform. Trains from London could also arrive here from the opposite direction, having undergone a circuitous route involving Edge Hill, the LNWR Bootle branch, the L&Y Southport line branching off east at Marsh Lane, and Sefton Junction. The Liverpool Overhead Railway train started its journey at Dingle, travelling past the docks to arrive at Aintree. Usually, trains went to Seaforth & Litherland station, but this special will have gone via the North Mersey branch and Sefton Junction. The other face of the island platform is where electric trains from

Exchange station would arrive. On Grand National day (only) some specials took the North Mersey branch from Rimrose Rd Junction to Sefton Junction and so to here, all at half speed because of the voltage difference. Aintree Central, on the Cheshire Lines, was very close, with the two systems connected north of here at Southport and Aintree Junctions. *(R Stephens)*

Aintree Sorting Sidings, 1961. The L&Y serviced trains between passengers arriving and departing by emptying some of the sorting sidings of goods wagons, and marshalling coaches in them. Putting up a great deal of smoke as they wait are (from the left) 78061 as a pilot for Patriot 45530, 42864 acting similarly to Jubilee 45586, and another Patriot 45534 on the right. The L&Y advertised trains from Manchester every 20 minutes from 10.40am until 12.40pm for the Friday race meeting here; the fare was 3s 6d (17½p). In the early 1930s, around 60 special trains ran on Grand National day, requiring 90 engines to haul them in 1934. In 2007, around 80,000 people attended the Grand National, only a small fraction arriving by train. *(JA Peden)*

Aintree Shed, 1959. The shed dates from just after the opening of the sidings in 1886, before which Sandhills shed (later called Bank Hall) serviced engines. It was built as a straight 8-road shed, No 19 in the L&Y system. In 1937, concrete *louvre* smoke vents replaced the roof. Other additions were an ash plant and a concrete mechanical coaling tower. This picture shows a wagon hoisted up the side of the tower, its contents going into a bunker under which engines positioned themselves for their tenders to be replenished. 0-6-0 goods engine No 52311 and a Hughes-Fowler "Crab" have had their fill. With 99% of the shed's allocation for freight, Grand National days saw a lot of passenger engines serviced before returning to the sorting sidings for their homeward journeys. The Cheshire Lines serviced its Grand National trains at Walton shed. *(BPC)*

Meanwhile, Back on the Main Line...

Kirkby Troughs, 1959. This view from Glover's Brow bridge sees Stanier 8F 2-8-0 No 48509 taking a train of coal empties, probably to Yorkshire, for refilling on 11th September. Slightly west of the station, the L&Y established a set of water troughs, whose purpose was to reduce the turnaround times at terminal stations as the engine would be partially serviced; the troughs were heated in cold weather. If the scoop wasn't retracted quickly enough, excess water would tend to wash away the ballast, so at some places there were sleepers laid longitudinally around the lines to prevent it. *(G Kaye)*

Kirkby Station, 1959. Heading east on 29th January is an express destined for Manchester, hauled by Jubilee class 4-6-0 No 45717 *Dauntless*. The down signals are elevated to allow them to be seen above the road bridge at the station, and having lower repeater arms for trains in the station. The start of the troughs can just be made out on the Liverpool line. Today it is hard to believe that during the celebrated 40-minute runs between the two cities, trains would charge through here at up to 75mph. *(G Kaye)*

Kirkby Station, 1954. This view is looking south towards Liverpool. There is a small stone booking office, with typical L&Y station clock, on the adjacent Glover's Brow bridge with a ramp to the down platform where there was this wooden waiting room. Steps led to the up platform, which had a small shelter on it. The platforms were staggered (the up one can just be seen under the road bridge), and the lamps had the station's name on the glass. Just leaving with a train to Wigan is Stanier 2-6-4T No 42284. A well-used goods yard is to the right, complete with a crane capable of lifting up to 5 tons. Through, and above, the bridge can be seen the home signal. The safety practice of painting the platform edges white, enforced in the war years, has persisted. From 1977, the station became a double terminus for the Merseyside 3rd-rail EMUs going back and forth to Liverpool from an extended down platform under the bridge. Meanwhile, from this end of the old down platform, DMUs plied their trade to and from Wigan, on their way to Rochdale, but now run via Manchester. *(JA Peden)*

Kirkby Station, 1965. A water softening plant used a chemical reaction to remove any hardness from the water, redundant locomotive tenders being used to remove the sludge. *(Lancashire & Yorkshire Railway Society)*

East of Kirkby, 1958.
Having been given the road, Austerity 2-8-0 No 90101 proceeds eastwards towards Liverpool with a short freight train. In August 1866 the L&Y opened its North Mersey Branch from Fazakerley Junction, about a mile west of here. Land north of the line was bought and between the East Junction on the main line, and the West Junction on the North Mersey Branch, about fifty loops were installed in two groups covering almost a mile, and were developed to assist with the sorting of wagons from the Liverpool's docks, factories and stores. The building in the background is a pumping station for St Helens Corporation Water Works. *(BPC)*

Dale Lane Sidings.
Many redundant steam engines were stored here after 1968 to await their turn at the torch. Here, minus coupling rods, is an example of the last true engine of Horwich design. *(BPC)*

Opposite page: Royal Ordnance Factory, Kirkby, 1945. A huge (743 acres) complex was hastily built here from September 1940. At its peak towards the end of World War II, something like 20,000 people (mostly women) worked here, and there was an internal rail system of some 19 miles.

Top: Station. A short branch and a passenger platform were built near the connection with the main line. There were three trains from Liverpool every shift, and bus and tram routes were extended from Liverpool as well. To confuse potential saboteurs, they had the destination "Simonswood" on the front.

Bottom: Loading Bay. In the buildings, all manner of wartime activities took place – parts were made by machines, and shells, mines and ammunition were filled, the finished goods being loaded into wagons. Engines such as "Pug" No 11246 saw in the New Year of 1941 doing shunting. Acquired by Liverpool Corporation in 1947, it soon became a vast employment area with over 120 firms from a wide range of backgrounds offering employment to 15,000 people. From 1952, a massive house building programme was developed locally to relieve congestion and overcrowding, and to help repair war damage in Liverpool. *(Both Knowsley Library Service)*

Simonswood, 1940. Starting here, and extending east for just over a mile, were up and down goods loops, completed in 1905. The eastern end was controlled by Rainford Colliery box, which had connections to Lord Derby's sidings until the 1930s. Between 1940 and 1942, a War Department siding was put in for a storage depot for munitions manufactured at Kirkby ROF. The western end of the loops was controlled by a small wooden box dating from 1884, but this was replaced from December 1940 by one of ARP design, similar to Wigan No 1 and Wallgate boxes. This view across the running lines (admittedly of very poor quality, but taken under wartime conditions) shows the 40-lever box with two smoke stacks, suggesting that it was probably a nice warm box to operate until its closure on 4th May 1965. The land here is very fertile with potatoes being the chief crop. *(BPC)*

Rainford Junction, 1956. Although planned by the Liverpool & Bury Railway, Rainford was opened by the L&Y on 20th November 1848. It closed almost ten years later, only to re-open here so that it could accommodate the branches from the north and south. This view of the junction is from the footbridge looking west towards Liverpool, and shows the Ormskirk branch from the north (right) and the line off south to St Helens. In the distance is the line (left) from Randle Junction on the St Helens line, to Bushy Lane Junction (right) on the Ormskirk line allowing through running towards Widnes and the docks there and at Garston. The platforms were of such a length that passengers could transfer between main and branch trains by simply walking along the platform. While the brick base of the signalbox is the original L&Y structure,

the top was rebuilt by the LMS in 1933. Now only 10 of its 56 levers are in use, with the line towards Liverpool having been singled from Fazakerley in 1970 and truncated at Kirkby to coincide with electrification seven years later. Two-car DMUs now ply the route, with a token being exchanged at the box for passage along the old up line. With nice straight track it is easy to see why L&Y expresses between the two counties use to storm through here.
(Lancashire & Yorkshire Railway Society)

Rainford Junction, 1956. A guest at the adjacent Junction Hotel just before mid-day on an April Saturday would have seen this train pass under New Lane bridge. Leaving the main line platform bound for Liverpool, is Stanier 2-6-4T No 42642 with a train from Wigan. If this was the 3.45pm from Bolton to Liverpool Exchange, arriving at 5pm, there were plenty of opportunities for interchange at Rainford. Passengers to and from both Ormskirk and St Helens could have reached their destinations. With such stopping trains approximately every two hours, this type of service should have been standard, but alas it was a rarity, so passengers preferred to use buses and cars. This, together with the decline in mining, led to the run down in services. As a nice touch "LMR" is written in whitewashed stone. *(RAS)*

Rainford connections, 1950s. Rainford became a junction when the line to St Helens was opened on 1st February 1858 by the St Helens & Runcorn Gap Railway. This enabled trains from the local pits to get to St Helens, and then to Widnes and Garston docks. Here, Ivatt 2-6-2T No 41286 waits on the curved, extended platforms having brought a train from the glass-making town. Being autofitted it will return without turning round. The line closed to passengers in 1951. On the northern side of the station was the site of the East Lancashire Railway line from Ormskirk, opened on 1st March 1858. Aintree-based Ivatt 2-6-2T No 41283 is waiting in the bay before going north. This service was one of several from that town to serve rudimentary halts along the line by railmotors. This style of service lasted from 1906 until the 1930s when Aspinall 2-4-2T autofitted trains took over and became colloquially known as the "Skem Dodger". In the last days of the L&Y, the pattern of service was a shuttle – leaving Ormskirk at 6.30am, the train would ply its route to Rainford Junction and back, the last train being at 10.40pm back to "home". Periodically throughout the day, it would re-coal at Ormskirk, but the service ceased in November 1956. Although advertised by a board on the coach's roof as "Ormskirk Rainford Junction & St. Helens" it was not a through service. The L&Y and LNWR services were separate, connections taking place at the junction station here. In 1973, the station dropped any pretence of being a junction.

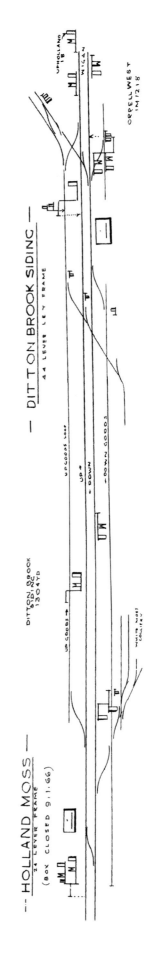

Holland Moss, 1956 and Ditton Brook Sidings. Having built its direct line, the L&Y found that the general increase in trade in the late Victorian age led to bottlenecks further along the line. Also, the L&Y wished to speed up its passenger services, which meant extra accommodation was required for slower moving freight trains. The 1899 Act provided for this in stages, and this was to be one of the places affected. Controlling the western ends of the loops, and the connections to Holland colliery, was the small (24-lever) Holland Moss signalbox. Looking east we see a train signalled to pass along the main line; it was probably taken on a Sunday when many such boxes were switched out. In the distance is the next box along the line – Ditton Brook Sidings. In fact, the top signals would have been operated by the nearest box and the lower distant arms by the next one in front. Ditton Brook, ¾ mile away, used its 44 levers to control the goods loops and sorting sidings. *(Both CHA Townley. Signalbox diagram courtesy of The Signalling Record Society)*

Upholland Station, 1972.
The L&Y opened this station west of the tunnel under the name Pimbo Lane, and Upholland station was opened to the east of the tunnel. In 1852, the latter station failed to appear in the timetable, and its name was transferred to what was Pimbo Lane station. This view is of the platform for Liverpool-bound passengers. The waiting room has a nicely arched entrance, and there is the obligatory station clock. Steps led down to the platforms from the bridge to the brick buildings (or wooden ones for Wigan passengers) both platforms having booking facilities.

(Today it's done on the train.) In the 1970s, the nameboards proclaimed, "Alight here for Skelmersdale New Town". *(JA Sommerfield)*

Upholland Tunnel. The only way to overcome the solid outcrop of rock was to build this 959-yard tunnel. The last seven miles from Liverpool were at an ever-stiffening gradient, the last two miles from Rainford Junction being at least 1 in 118. L&Y Acts of 1899 included powers to build a second tunnel here. However, the expense meant that the bottleneck was a problem to be addressed "later", but the intervention of the World War I meant that this was "never". *(D Ibbotson)*

Above: West of Orrell Station, 1961. Having passed under the bridge, the 11.30am from Liverpool Exchange is passing the compact goods yard. Class 5 4-6-0 No 44695 of Low Moor shed has been signalled by the 60-lever signalbox visible over the coaches. After travelling to Halifax, the front coaches will arrive at 2.00pm at Leeds Central, while the rear coaches will go to Bradford Exchange, and arrive two minutes later. *(AC Gilbert)*

Opposite page, top: West of Orrell Station, 1961. At the station end of the goods yard is another bridge over the railway line, and no doubt the passengers will be in eager anticipation of a good day at Aintree's Grand National. The train engine is Patriot class 4-6-0 No 45534 *E. Tootal Broadhurst*. Helping to maintain the schedule, as well as providing route knowledge, is LMS class 2P 4-4-0 No 40684. Note the old coach body in use as an office and mess room by the local coal merchant. *(AC Gilbert)*

West of Orrell Station, 1953. Class 5 4-6-0 No 44702 has been toiling up the gradient from Wigan for the last 4-mile stretch – two of them at 1 in 91, but thankfully, the crest and Upholland Tunnel is ahead. The rear coaches are passing through Orrell station with its short loops and freight facilities on both sides of the line. The three arms on the post by the road bridge are to allow shunting into these facilities – the top arm being for the loop on the down side, the middle arm for transference to the up main, and the lower arm for access the up loops. *(BPC)*

Orrell Station 1971. Even though there was an adjacent road bridge, a covered footbridge was provided as well. This leads from a booking office of typical L&Y two-colour design. The Wigan-bound passengers had the benefit of a substantial wooden shelter, complete with fireplaces. There were fewer passengers expected in the Liverpool direction, hence the bus stop shelter. *(JA Sommerfield)*

Orrell Station, 1971. This was one of the original stations on the Liverpool & Bury Railway line, almost four miles from Wigan. It was renamed "Orrell and Upholland" on 1st September 1882, only to revert to the shorter name on 13th October 1900. Looking towards Wigan, note how the steps end almost under the canopy of the shelters. This would allow continuous passenger protection in the rain. *(JA Sommerfield)*

Orrell East, 1953. Passing along the down main is class 7F 0-8-0, No 49552, hauling a mixed train. The L&Y's 1899 Act was for the widening of its lines from Walton Junction to Pemberton Junction, to be done in stages as loops between Ditton Brook and Holland Moss, Rainford Colliery and Simonswood, and Orrell and Pemberton (the latter opening in 1904). The signals protecting the merger of the main and loop lines stand out to the rear with the parachute water tank for the loop line. *(BPC)*

Orrell Loops, 1951. The main line is signalled for a train to pass towards Liverpool. Consequently, as the lines narrow from four to two, another train has to wait for a clear road after the train on the main line has passed. The footplate staff of Hughes-Fowler "Crab" 2-6-0 No 42856 enjoy the May sunshine, but they will need to exercise all their skills in effectively doing a "hill start". While most of the coal used in this country today is for the generation of electricity, it wasn't always so, as the gas, domestic and industrial markets were more important then. Fifty years ago we were mining 240 million tons a year, half of it delivered by train. *(BPC)*

Orrell Main Line, c1920s. Hauling an express for Liverpool from Leeds Central is an unidentified 1400 Class 4-4-2. Its speed would probably be down to around 40mph, but this would be offset by previously attaining 75mph along parts of the direct line and the descent from Orrell tunnel towards its destination. While its 7ft 3in driving wheels were great for fast running, it would have needed a footplate crew of some experience to maintain the timetable up this 1 in 91 gradient. In retrospect, perhaps more (six) smaller (6ft) driving wheels would have increased the adhesion of the engine, so allowing better performance over such a graded line. Fears at the time of their introduction regarding stability when at speed on curves were unfounded. *(ES Cox)*

Winstanley Colliery Sidings, 1961. While Orrell East signalbox was at the down end of the loops, ¾ mile to the east was this 25 lever box, built in around 1947 by the LMS, which controlled events at the up end. Passing towards Liverpool is Stanier 8F 2-8-0 No 48515 on 4th November. The top pair of red home arms is controlled by this signalbox using levers 25 and 23. The lower pair, yellow distant arms would be operated by the box in front, Pemberton Junction. Notice in the distance, the next signal for up trains consisting of splitting distants – left for Wigan and right for the avoiding line. *(AC Gilbert)*

Winstanley Colliery Sidings, 1951. There was a loop on the up side too. Beyond the eastern end of the loops there were two lines through Pemberton station, so trains had to wait their turn. With a descending gradient, stopping an unfitted freight train needed a high degree of skill, especially if the engine was to take on water as (like at the Orrell end on the down side) a water tank was provided. Doing exactly that is a member of the footplate crew of 0-8-0 No 49563 in the up loop. Passing along the up main line is sister engine No 49582 with an empty train. *(RAS)*

Pemberton Station Entrance, 1966. No grand statement here – simply a small building at street level with this uninviting entrance. Company style brickwork was used, but the whole station has now been completely rebuilt to encourage passengers for trains to and from Kirkby and to Rochdale via Manchester. *(Lancashire & Yorkshire Railway Society)*

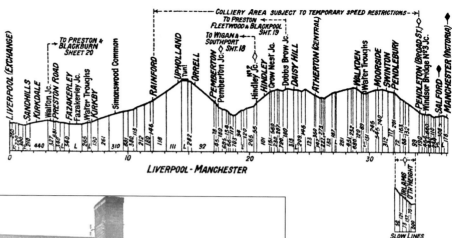

Right: Pemberton Station Looking East, 1964. An excursion from Bridlington to Blackpool rounds the curve from Wigan Wallgate into Pemberton station on 22nd August. Having reduced speed for the junction with the avoiding line, the footplate staff of Jubilee 4-6-0 No 45739 *Ulster* require enough speed to take the engine up to the top of the gradient. Extensive mining in the area meant a speed restriction was imposed on trains passing through. For all the fast work on the direct line, and the race across west Lancashire to Liverpool, speeds were very limited here. *(BPC)*

Right: Pemberton Station, 1961. Trundling east through the station is a trainload of empty mineral wagons. Class 4F 0-6-0 No 44094 has been in charge since it left Fazakerley sidings, its destination being Crofton colliery in Yorkshire. As the brakes of the wagons are connected to those of the engine, the train can to travel faster than a non-fitted one. The right-hand pair of signals is for the line to Wigan Wallgate, while the train will take the avoiding line via Westwood Park. At Nationalisation, coal output was 187.5 million tons a year, but 60 years later it struggles to be 10% of this figure. *(BPC)*

Pemberton Station Looking West, 1976. This small station opened with the line in 1848. Access is from the adjacent road to the upper storey of the station buildings, and steps lead out onto a footbridge with more leading down to the platforms. A small wooden shelter is for Liverpool-bound passengers, while the Wigan platform has more facilities in a brick building complete with station clock. *(ND Mundy)*

Wigan's Avoiding Line, 1966. Opened in 1889 (1st May for goods, and a month later for passengers) the Pemberton loop passed from Pemberton in the west to Hindley in the east. Being constructed late in the history of railways, it crossed many other pieces of transport infrastructure. Here, the loop is curving away, entirely on embankments (built from dirt from the nearby LNWR-connected Crow Orchard colliery) with 25 bridges. First, it crosses the Leeds-Liverpool canal, then in quick succession, the LNWR main quadruple line near Springs Branch, then the branch itself (on a 147ft bridge) and finally the GCR line to Wigan Central. Crow Orchard colliery closed in 1904 and become a coal yard. The "switchback" (named because of a dip in the middle) allowed express trains to save around 10 minutes by avoiding Wallgate station, so the L&Y could compete for the Lancashire-Yorkshire traffic even though its route was longer and more steeply graded. Freight trains were also sent along this route to avoid the Wigan station area. Ince Moss colliery connected with the line, with loops and sidings being put down at Westwood Park, approximately half way along the loop, and lasting until the end of 1944, being finally removed in 1952. Looking east from Little Lane Bridge in Pemberton, this view shows signal posts of different designs, the avoiding line's post having a lower repeater arm. The avoiding line closed on July 14th 1969. *(Lancashire & Yorkshire Railway Society)*

Wigan Wallgate Signalbox, 1984. Curving in on a viaduct, the Liverpool line (behind the signal box) is met from the north by the line from Southport (in front). Both lines then pass under the West Coast Main Line. In the fork created by the meeting of these two lines, and built of material to render it blast-proof, is this 1941 modern-image box, still in use. In addition to an internal staircase, it has 14in solid brick walls, 12in reinforced flat roof and no locking room windows. When it was commissioned, it took over the duties of No 3 box from the east, as well as No 5 box along the Southport line, and No 4 and Worsley Mesnes boxes, on the Liverpool line. In total, the 6 men at the new box replaced 14 men and 2 boys. Although of "state of the art" design, it looks dark and barren, as befits the period. For the number of boxes that it replaced, 75 levers and 39 key switches for signals is not large, but some of the redundant boxes were very small. *(G Earl)*

Wigan Engine Shed. West of the junction of the Southport and Liverpool lines, and a short way along the former, was the site of Wigan's engine shed – No 16 in the L&Y system. The first shed, of 1860, was rebuilt in mid-1877, enlarged less than ten years later, and closed in 1905 due to subsidence. A larger, newer one at Prescott Street was opened, with 14 roads each 18 bays long, but it too suffered from the same problem, and the front quarter was removed soon after the end of World War II leaving an odd L-shaped building.

Top left: 1935. Adjacent to a typical company water column at LMS shed 23D is a smartly turned out member of a very numerous class. 38 years previously, Aspinall 0-6-0 goods engine No 12360 had been L&Y No 465, and it would remain in active service for another 28 years. Reasons for their longevity were a simple design to start with and cheapness to maintain. The capacity of the tender was 1,600 gallons, and when asked about the small size Aspinall replied, "on account of the well known apparatus invented by Mr J Ramsbottom. Water is picked up from troughs between the rails ... relieving engines from hauling the extra load ... (it) prevents serious blockage on a line." *(WL Good)*

Top right: 1950. Looking into the removed section of BR shed 27D this view shows an engine designed to cope with long-distance coal trains, for which many companies developed the 0-8-0 wheel arrangement. In April 1900, Aspinall designed an engine capable of pulling almost half as much again as the 0-6-0 engines. A development of them was the type pictured here with a large boiler and superheater. Note the 8-wheel tender as well. With many trains spending a lot of time in loops waiting for a pathway, there was the risk of running out of water, so the tender capacity was increased from 2,290 gallons to 3,600 gallons. No 52782 was of 1903 vintage, and would be withdrawn in September 1950. *(BPC)*

Bottom left: 1951. This engine, No 51319, started life as a 0-6-0 goods tender engine No 561, introduced by Barton Wright in 1877. With Aspinall's more powerful 0-6-0 locomotives becoming more plentiful from 1890, the decision was made not to scrap these engines, but to convert them. The method was to fit a saddle tank over the boiler, lengthen the rear main frame a little to accommodate the bunker, and fit a cab over the footplate, so in August 1891 this engine emerged as a tank locomotive. This proved to be a good idea based on a well-planned engine, many lasting well over 50 years as conversions, and the last one surviving until 1964. Their size and power made them useful engines for the sorting sidings in the south Lancashire area. This one was withdrawn in 1959. *(TG Wassell)*

Bottom right: 1963. Filling the tenders of engines with coal was a soul-destroying and back-breaking job undertaken in all weathers – usually in the open. While Wigan wasn't important enough to be allocated a proper coaling facility, it did warrant two of these portable conveyor belts (or "elevators"). Here one is being used to top up a Fairburn 2-6-4T locomotive's fuel supply on 3rd June. *(J Alsop)*

Wallgate Station, 1967.
This is looking east from the carriage sidings north of the LNWR station, which served the West Coast Main Line. The station consisted of a single island, and avoiding loops in both directions, with a bay at the Southport end. To the south was a loading bay and sidings for storing stock. On the extreme left a road slopes down to the site of the old station. A DMU stopping train waits in the down platform, and simmering in the sidings is the station pilot. It cost £94 to build the servicing facilities for this in June 1911, as the use of

continuous pilot meant that the engine was away from its home shed for longer than a day, with loco crews signing on and off here. Adjacent is a small (50ft diameter) turntable, as the loco depot was some distance away to the west. *(RK Blencowe)*

Wigan Wallgate, 1965.
Having left Liverpool Exchange 50 minutes previously, the time is now getting close to 1.30pm as a train arrives in the up platform at Wallgate station. It will have stopped at all the stations *en-route* and will continue in this vein as it proceeds to Rochdale, arriving in an hour's time. With Manchester to Yorkshire expresses stopping at Rochdale, passenger transfers were possible. Both engines in the picture were designed by Ivatt. On the right is class 2 2-6-0 No 46497, while on the left is fellow 2-6-0 No 43019 having brought an excursion (probably from Southport)

into the bay. Note the two parachute water tanks on the down side. *(HC Casserley)*

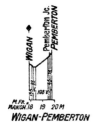

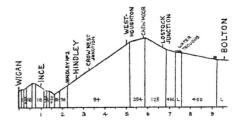

Wallgate Station Entrance, 1966. The original 1848 station, described as "a hovel" in the *Railway Times* of 2nd June 1860, was east of Wallgate and was replaced by one to the west of the road that year. This had its access to the north from Droning Street, and to the south along a long lane from Wallgate. It consisted of two platforms, joined by a wide curved passageway. To compete with the new LNWR station opened in 1894, the L&Y enlarged and rebuilt its station a short distance to the east, and closer to the town centre. When the station's anniversary came along, the buildings were instantly recognisable, but cars and street paraphernalia now dominate the visual scene. While architecturally it was unlikely to win an award, the style is indicative of a way of life – footway access and a fair-sized covered area for passenger protection. On entering the building, there was a booking office and a wide set of steps down to the single island platform. Up to 1924, it was known as the L&Y station, and only when both stations were under the control of the LMS was "Wallgate" added. *(Lancashire & Yorkshire Railway Society)*

Under Wallgate. Emerging from the road bridge across the lines is an up freight train hauled by Stanier 2-6-0 No 42957. This small class of engines was his first after his appointment as CME in 1932. With the success of the Hughes-Fowler "Crabs", his design was probably unnecessary, but perhaps he wanted to establish his credentials with the LMS, having come from their rivals the GWR. To the right is a big water tank and what use to be Wigan L&Y No 2 signalbox, which closed when the area was resignalled, in 1941. The next year, the winter blizzards were so strong that the line here was blocked from 19th to 23rd January. *(BPC)*

Going Down to Wallgate, c1950s. With the LNWR station on the right and the L&Y goods shed on the left, 2-6-4T No 42115 threads its way down under the photographer standing on King Street footbridge and along the slope to go under Wallgate to the L&Y passenger station. It is an excursion, probably bound for Southport or Liverpool. Both the engine and the coaches have an identification number on them, so that for the return journey they can be reunited. *(BKB Green)*

North Western Yard Pilot, 1966. Even though the LNWR lines pass over those of the L&Y at the western end of Wallgate station, a short distance east of the station the lines are next to each other. The space between the two company's lines was utilised by the LNWR for coaches and parcels stock. Here, Ivatt 2-6-0 No 43033 sorts out the stock as station pilot. King Street footbridge crosses the L&Y lines, and the LNWR sidings. Now a collector's item, a Ford Anglia 105E is in the foreground. *(G Coltas)*

Coming Up From Wallgate, 1947. While the L&Y is famous for its 0-8-0 engines, they are usually remembered as being rather massive, with the boiler appearing to be out of proportion to the frames. Several members of the class are illustrated in this volume, but their small-boilered relatives are featured comparatively rarely. Waiting adjacent to the lines that pass down under Wallgate to arrive at the town's L&Y station is No 12727 on 9th August. The first well-loaded coal wagon appears to belong to T Cheetham & Co from Fazakerley. *(AJ Bryant)*

Arriving at Wigan, 1961. Going west, the line rises continuously to enable it to pass over the Leeds & Liverpool canal. This puts the L&Y adjacent to, and level with, the LNWR lines, so exchanges were possible between them. Passengers could leave either Wallgate or North Western stations, and arrive at Manchester. Two days before Christmas we witness a train arriving along the L&Y line, and about to pass down to Wallgate station. In charge is Stanier 2-6-4T No 42612. *(BPC)*

Wigan No 1 Signalbox, 1971. The line to Manchester passes on the far side of Wigan No 1 signalbox, and can be seen rising to cross the Leeds & Liverpool canal to the right of it. The construction was of Air-Raid Precautions (ARP) design and dates from the 1941 resignalling scheme, replacing several large boxes in the area. It mostly controlled the LNWR lines, and the L&Y line from Ince almost to Wallgate station. It too was replaced in 1972 by Warrington power signalbox, some seven miles south. *(ND Mundy)*

Ince Station, 1951. A little over a mile from Wigan, the line goes under Green Lane. Looking towards Wigan, this view shows the station offices with a station clock over the timetable noticeboard. The wagons in the centre are on the connections to Ince Hall colliery; there was an up loop there as well. In 1918, a bomb from a Zeppelin fell through the roof and floor of Ince Hall signalbox, but fortunately it didn't explode. In the early 1870s there were 76 coke ovens working here, Ince being one of the most prolific areas for coal production at that time. It was also famous for its wagon works. *(Stations UK)*

Ince Station, 1966. The island platform station replaced an 1860s station in 1894. This view towards Hindley, shows the wide covered access from the road bridge. The L&Y signalbox, on the down side, with its 24-lever tappet frame, survived until 1st October 1972. The line on the right is the down goods loop. Note how the railway rises to pass over the Ince Hall branch of the Leeds & Liverpool canal. It cost £192,000 to refurbish the footbridge in 2006. *(Lancashire & Yorkshire Railway Society)*

Near Hindley No 2 Signalbox, 1961. Having left Southport about 30 minutes ago on 16th September, class 5 4-6-0 No 44887 heads east to Manchester Victoria via Bolton, the roundabout route that existed before the building of the direct line. A little over ½ mile before, the train will have met the "Pemberton Loop", or Wigan avoiding line, at Hindley No 3 signalbox. There were extensive sidings, in both up and down directions. *(AC Gilbert)*

Hindley No 2 Signalbox, 1961. Many trains with coal from the numerous mines of the Wigan coalfield were assembled at Bamfurlong sorting sidings, south of the town alongside the LNWR main line. Trains could set off from there in many directions due to the numerous connecting lines. Sometimes trains were "topped & tailed" (that is, an engine was placed at each end due to the changes in direction that would be necessary). Such a train, bound for Kearsley power station near Bolton, had Jubilee 4-6-0 No 45600 *Bermuda* at one end. Here we see the train coming off the line from De Trafford Junction onto the main line assisted by LNWR 0-8-0 No 49451. Heading for the up loop, the train will probably stop by Hindley No 1 box, and this engine will be released to go back to the sorting sidings. *(AC Gilbert)*

Hindley No 2 Signalbox, 1965.
This was the meeting point and sorting out place for a variety of routes. From the west arrive the Wigan and Southport lines, as well as the Wigan avoiding line. Just under the gantry, curving away to the right, is the link north to meet the Lancashire Union Railway (the Whelley Loop) at De Trafford Junction. An excursion train ("The East Midlander", organised by the RCTS) is passing along the up slow line, probably in readiness for travelling towards Bolton at the next junction, Crow Nest. *(BG Barlow)*

West of Hindley, 1963.
Signalled to proceed on the up fast in readiness to pass along the direct line is an express from Liverpool. It is one of the approximately hourly services to the West Riding of Yorkshire, destined for Bradford and Leeds Central. At that time, 10-coach trains were commonplace, and hauling this train is grimy class 5 4-6-0 No 44951 not far from its place of building, Horwich. It has three more revenue earning days before being withdrawn at the age of twenty years. *(J Davenport)*

West of Hindley, 1961. At approximately 3.20pm on 16th September, looking towards Manchester from the fine wrought iron footbridge to the west of the station, and adjacent to the divergence north of the line to De Trafford Junction, we see Stanier 2-6-4T No 42363 heading along the down slow line with the 2.30pm from Rochdale to Wigan. This has arrived here via Bury and Bolton, meeting the direct line at Crow Nest Junction. At that point, both directions had loops, the down side having two, making seven running lines in addition to a set of sidings on the down side. *(Peter Hutchinson)*

West of Hindley, 1961. At approximately 3.55pm, the 3.12pm from Victoria to Southport leaves Hindley to make its way to Wigan. It will have stopped at all the stations on the direct line, and will stop at most of the stations on its run from Wigan to the seaside. The task will be well within the capabilities of Jubilee 4-6-0 No 45641 *Boscawen*. Peering out from underneath the bridge can just be seen the platforms of Hindley North station. The different arches of the bridge show the original lines, to the left, and the later fast lines. No 1 signalbox, which was resited from between the fast and slow lines in 1956, is partially hidden by the water tank. Waiting at the stop signals, before proceeding onto the up slow line, was a convenient place for engines to take on water.
(Peter Hutchinson)

West of Hindley, 1963. Heading west on the down fast line is an express from Bradford. Barely a teenager, engine No 44689 will take the train to Liverpool. Above the road bridge, the signals show that a train is expected along its parallel track, the down slow. To the right of the train are two down through sidings that branched from the fast line just this side of the bridge. On the right is a magnificent display of arms controlling goods movements. A set of 15 blind-ended sidings can be made out between the signal posts from the right-hand of these two sidings. After sorting, trains could pass to a variety of destinations – De Trafford, Wigan or Pemberton, hence the multiple arms on each post.
(J Davenport)

Hindley Station, early 1900s. Racing through on the up fast line is an express for Leeds via Manchester. Hauling this non-taxing train is one of Aspinall's "High-flyers", 4-4-2 No 1406. Built locally at Horwich in February 1902, it was allocated the LMS number 10321 before being withdrawn in 1931. In the background is the covered footbridge leading from the booking office on the left, to the platforms.
(J Ryan Collection)

Hindley Station Exterior, 1966. Opened on 20th November 1848 as a two platform station, it gained two more on the arrival of the Atherton line 40 years later. This is the main entrance from Ladies Lane with a booking office and a covered footbridge leading to the platforms. All four lines had passenger facilities, but now only Manchester-bound passengers have any shelter from the rain. On 1st July 1950, the station became "Hindley North", reverting to Hindley some 30 years later. In between, Hindley Green on the LNWR line from Wigan to Manchester had closed in 1961, and the GCR Hindley and Platt Bridge had changed to "Hindley South" in 1952 before closing in 1964. *(Lancashire & Yorkshire Railway Society)*

Crow Nest Junction, 1956. For 20 years this was just a place on the route to Bolton (the two lines nearest the box, on the left). Just over half a mile east of Hindley station was the site chosen in 1868 for the L&Y Hilton House branch. By this branch, the L&Y, and its allies, had a route to Preston and Blackburn, independent of the LNWR. 20 years later, the L&Y built four lines from Manchester (right of the signalbox). With 92 levers this was a large box built for the opening of the direct line. Above the levers are the block instruments with the line diagram suspended from the ceiling. Each numbered lever has a catch on its lower end, which is raised by the catch handle on the back of the lever. Only then can the lever be moved in the frame to alter the position of a signal (usually by wire) or a set of points (by rods). There were numerous facing point locks and 6 diamonds necessitating elaborate locking mechanisms below the frame. As services reduced due to the direct lines' contraction to two lines from 6th September 1965, followed by the closure of the Hilton House branch on 8th September, a simple double junction complete with new (1st October 1972) signalbox became sufficient. *(Signalling Record Society, Scrimgeour Collection)*

The Original Main Line, via Bolton.

This was promoted by the Manchester, Bolton & Bury Canal Navigation & Railway, who initially sought to close the canal and build a railway on its bed. However, they obtained another Act to build the railway alongside the canal, as Parliament encouraged competition. At that time, a traveller from Manchester to Preston and the north had to travel east to Parkside along the Liverpool & Manchester Railway, then north along the

North Union line. The route of the Bolton & Preston Railway, which opened throughout on 22nd June 1843, made the journey from Manchester to Preston 6 miles shorter, but the two companies (the NUR and the B&PR) amalgamated the next year. The traffic of the expanding port of Liverpool with Manchester and Yorkshire was in the hands of the original Liverpool & Manchester Railway, but in 1845, an Act was obtained by the Liverpool & Bury Railway in an attempt to break this

stranglehold. The line was to run from Liverpool by way of Wigan to meet the former Bolton & Preston Railway at Lostock, some three miles east of Bolton. At Bolton, trains could come from Manchester to pass to Liverpool. After passing through Bolton station, the line branched off east to Bury. Henceforth trains could continue east to Rochdale and meet the Manchester & Leeds Railway near Rochdale to gain access to Yorkshire. After absorption by the L&Y in 1846, the line to the west of Bolton was opened on 20th November 1848. Thus traffic from Salford could run on L&Y metals to Liverpool – albeit by a roundabout journey some 8¾ miles longer than its competitor from Ordsall Lane to Liverpool.

Top: Westhoughton Station, 1951. Originally, the station name was made up of two parts, but quite when they merged is uncertain. The taller, non-standard L&Y buildings are on the Bolton platform, but Wigan-bound passengers have more modest accommodation. Canopies were never provided for passenger protection. *(Stations UK)*

Westhoughton Station, 1966. Looking south from the overbridge, this view shows class 5 4-6-0 No 45070 hauling an express towards Bolton, having just passed through the station. On the other side of the bridge was the goods yard, complete with a 5-ton crane and facilities for livestock. The Metal Box Company had a sidings connection on the down side too, hence the name of the 24-lever signalbox. *(Lancashire & Yorkshire Railway Society)*

Chew Moor Sidings, c1961. An excursion, 1Z11, probably from Southport, heads north towards Bolton, pulled by a dirty class 5 4-6-0 No 45437 of 1937 vintage. To ensure that after servicing, the engine rejoined the correct coaches, both had the excursion number on them (note the piece of paper on the front of the first of the non-corridor coaches). Controlling the northern access to the up and down loops and the southern exit from the sidings is this L&Y 48-lever wooden signalbox of 1915 vintage. Behind the train are the southern accesses for the up and down loops, and beyond the bridge is Westhoughton station. The signal post is interesting. The top one (painted red on the other side) is the home signal for this box, and is operated by it. Beneath it, the yellow arm is operated by the box in front. *(T Heavyside)*

Chew Moor Sidings, 1963. About 50 yards north of the previous picture we see a train from the north. The time is about 2.40 on a sunny March afternoon, and a rare visitor, LNER class B1 4-6-0 No 61062, drifts down to the station with the 2.00pm stopping train from Manchester to Liverpool Exchange via Bolton, arriving at 3.41pm. In the background is a small cabin that housed four levers, and in the distance is the signalbox that controlled the northern access to the loops. A station existed in this area for just six months from January 1851 according to timetables. *(D Hampson)*

Chew Moor Sidings, 1964. Heading a trainload of vans in No 2 up goods siding is an unidentified Austerity 2-8-0 engine and on the adjacent line is a train of mineral wagons. Ahead of them are four loops with sidings beyond. There were sidings here for the receipt of manure until around 1900. Privies were in general use then in large towns like Bolton, and the night soil, as it was called, was collected from households and loaded onto trains in the town at Craddock Lane on the line to Blackburn. From the sidings here, it was delivered to farmers for use as manure. Note the parachute water tank for waiting engines to replenish their tanks. *(Lancashire & Yorkshire Railway Society)*

Lostock Sidings South, 1963. This 25-lever signalbox (just in the bottom-right of the picture) controlled the northern entrance to the loops, the southern entrance being at Chew Moor Sidings. From these loops were two sets of sidings. The Bolton to Preston line passes across the picture from right to left in the background. On 22nd January 1914, the L&Y board accepted the estimate of JW Pearce & Co (£35,354 12s 6d) for widening the Westhoughton connecting line and sidings at Lostock Junction, near Bolton. However, as

reported on 16th July that year, JW Pearce had gone into liquidation, so Thomas Wrigley offered to carry out the balance of the work at Lostock Junction, his tender for the whole contract having been £36,618 16s 5d. It appears that the box and the sidings were opened during the World War I in 1915. Although the curvature of the sidings would have been compatible with a connection with the main line in the distance, I have not found any evidence to support such a connection. Although extensive, their function isn't clear and they seemed to be most frequently used for storing disused stock. *(D Hampson)*

Lostock Junction Exterior, 1964. Originally there was a station serving the 1841 line from Bolton to Chorley, and the one at Preston was another two years away. However, soon after the opening of the line to Hindley in 1848, plans were drawn up for a station to serve both lines. The first station was too far north so another had to be built. This was done adjacent to a level crossing of the line, and opened in 1887. Due to the increased use of the line the Board of Trade encouraged the crossing to be made by means of a bridge, entailing a new entrance. As can be seen, the building is in-between the bridges for both lines, Hindley nearest us and Preston further away. When it was built, the company had developed a corporate image using bricks of two different colours for its booking offices. Uniquely, there is a water tank on top. *(Lancashire & Yorkshire Railway Society)*

Lostock Junction, 1951. Platform 1 (on the left) and 2 were for the line to Preston; note the water column at the end. The crossing that the bridge replaced was at the end of the platforms. The wheel has done a complete turn and now only Preston bound trains can stop at the station. *(Stations UK)*

Lostock Junction, 1959. Looking towards Bolton from the road bridge in August, is the goods yard with a fair number of wagons in it – probably surplus stock in storage. Although essentially a rural community, the goods shed (from 1899) was large. Extra sidings were added to the goods yard in World War I, and in the distance is the large, 90-lever signalbox of similar vintage controlling the westerly separation into two routes and the easterly organisation of traffic onto quadruple lines for the run into Bolton. Notice the speed restriction (60mph) and the new signals on a much shorter post. *(D Hampson)*

Deane Lane Water Troughs Lostock, c1899. A fascinating picture of the line under construction with a Wigan-bound train taking water from the troughs. Prior to filling, the tanks would have been full of air, and if this could not be vented quickly enough, the tanks could be damaged. Radial tanks had four venting pipes in the corner of the cab, so when the tanks were full, the water overflowed through these pipes – an incentive for the fireman to be precise looking at the water gauge, and operating the mechanism to retract the scoop! A water tank to supply the troughs can be seen above the coaches. Construction of the new lines has produced the up line with the sleepers for the down line lying in waiting. The "X" on a signal arm meant that it wasn't in use. This down train is running over the intended up slow line after the work is finished. *(BPC)*

Deane Lane Water Troughs c1899. Signalled to take the Preston line at the junction ahead is a "High Flyer" 4-4-2 as built. The trailing axle had inside bearings, which some believed contributed to the engines less-than-smooth running. Consequently, the bearings were moved to the outside of the wheels, and their riding was much improved. It was a few years before two lamps on the buffer beam signified an express train. *(LGRP)*

Deane Lane Water Troughs Lostock, c1960. Heading west is an excursion from Rochdale for Southport accompanied by the River Croal; in charge is Hughes-Fowler 2-6-0 No 42704. Taking the Hindley line at the junction ahead, the train will pass via Wigan *en-route* to the seaside. The L&Y hoped that the new direct line would reduce the pressure on this section of line, but it didn't. Consequently, they added two extra lines to the south of the existing pair for a distance of just over 2¼ miles from the junction to Bullfield, on the outskirts of Bolton. These opened in 1899 at a cost of £38,634. The lines were paired, up to the north and down to the south. Following quadrupling, these troughs of 504 yards in length were extended to the slow lines; they were heated in frosty weather. *(J Davenport)*

Deane Lane Water Troughs Lostock, 1957. Jubilee 4-6-0 No 45698 *Mars*, in charge of eleven coaches, takes on water. Unfortunately smoke obscures parts of a wonderful signal gantry for the down lines. The four signals are all distant signals for the junction ahead. The pair on the left for the slow line shows the Wigan route to be the main destination hence the height of the post. In contrast, most of the fast line's trains would take the Preston line, so its Wigan arm is lower down. The engine's tender isn't its intended partner – that went to Royal Scot No 6166, this engine receiving the smaller 3,500 gallon Midland Railway style one. *(BKB Green)*

Shunting Around Bolton, 1951. Not only were there numerous sidings and goods sheds south of the L&Y station in the town, but there were some to the east as well. Just after the River Croal passed under the line in the Bullfield area, the L&Y developed some sidings from 1860. The main traffic was material for road construction, Bolton Corporation having yards at Wellington and Mayor Streets. Typical of the engines that would have shunted wagons in such sidings around the town (like here along the Manchester Road) is this Barton Wright 0-6-0ST No 51513, seen on 24th April. Note the sheeted wagons, a common practice to prevent the weather getting at loads in open wagons. However, as reported to the L&Y Board in 1856, there were risks, as a loose wagon cover killed a platelayer, for which the company were liable. They blamed the night-man for not checking that the cover was secure. *(HC Casserley)*

Bullfield, 1957. An accident here in 1957 was as a result of the arrangements in force to deliver coal to signalboxes. An engine was waiting on the down slow while coal from its train was unloaded at Bullfield West signalbox. Unfortunately, the driver hadn't pulled forward far enough, and the brake van and wagon were fouling the points that allow down fast to down slow line transfers to take place. Consequently, when the 2.00pm for Liverpool (1.18pm ex-Rochdale) tried to perform that

manoeuvre, it struck the offending coal wagon. As reported in the Bolton Evening News on 19th January, "The engine of the express was separated from its coaches and doors and woodwork were ripped from compartments. The tender left the rails and crashed into the signalbox." Passengers in the first carriage of the Rochdale train were thrown to the floor by the crash, and the box was left at a precarious angle, but fortunately, no one was injured. Track circuiting would have told the signalman that the line was occupied and prevented this. A wooden replacement box opened two months later, and lasted until 1990. *(Bolton Evening News and F Collinge Collection)*

Bullfield. The gradient is down at 1 in 271 from Bullfield West box, easing to 1 in 398 to Bolton. Bullfield East signalbox was north of the four running lines, with Austerity 2-8-0 No 90310 peering out from one of the loops behind it. This 1905 box took over the duties of both Bullfield No 1 and No 2 boxes, and was built so that it could be extended later, but this never happened. Above the box are the Spa Road gas holders with a typical wagon for delivery of coal on the right.

Bolton Gas Works, 1958. To the north of the line, adjacent to Spa Fields, the Corporation took over the gas works from 1872, and they soon became rail connected. Later, there was also an electricity works, which received its coal via the same sidings. The sharp curves meant that only short wheelbase engines could work the sidings, so the North Western Gas Board hired "Pug" No 51232 during 1957-8 from Bank Hall shed, although usually, the Gas Board's own 0-4-0ST engines (named *Alderman Webster* and *Glaister*) shunted the site. *(CB Golding)*

Dawes Street, Bolton, 1963. The widened line was opened between Bullfield and Lostock on 28th December 1899, seven years before the section from Trinity Street to here was opened on 10th April 1906, at a cost of £49,789. Extensive tunnelling (77yd) and bridge building was necessary with the new pair of lines to the south of the existing pair. This is the view from the LNWR coal drops at its passenger station. Class 8F 2-8-0 No 48164 is heading east, and is about to go under Dawes Street with an up freight. The colour lights have recently replaced a fine array of seven posts with small arms dating from the widening. *(D Hampson)*

Bolton, c1939. On Tuesday 29th May 1838, a railway line opened from New Bailey Street in Salford to Bolton promoted by the Manchester, Bolton & Bury Canal Navigation & Railway (although the railway never actually went to Bury nor Manchester). The terminus in Bolton was between two bridges of Bridgeman Street and Trinity Street. Five years later, a line was opened north from Bolton towards Euxton, where it joined the North Union Railway heading north to Preston. The platforms on the west of the station were later

extended under Trinity Street. Rounding the curve under Johnson Street footbridge, is a stopping passenger train that has just passed under Newport Street bridge ready to stop at the station behind us. There is a fascinating range of L&Y lower quadrant signals for both directions, all controlled by Bolton West box, to the right of the picture. The need for track circuiting was demonstrated here in August 1963 (the white diamond on the signal post indicates that the presence of a train will be indicated in the signalbox). A light engine was taking water at the water column seen under the footbridge on the down through line, but it appears to have been "forgotten" by the signalman, and another train was sent along the line. Fortunately, the second train consisted of empty stock and although there was some damage and disruption, no injuries were reported. *(Stations UK)*

Bolton, 1962. Creeping out of Bradshawgate tunnel and past the empty Byng Street carriage sidings is a train on the line from Blackburn. Completed to Hellifield in 1880, it became the route for the Midland Railway service to Scotland two years later. The train pictured is one of three a day with carriages between Colne and London Euston. Class 5 4-6-0 No 45209 is slowing down in readiness to stop at Trinity Street station. The lines to the left met the line from Trinity Street station to create a triangle that was useful for turning engines, and sometimes, complete trains. *(D Hampson)*

Bolton, Trinity Street Bridge, 1956.
Looking south from Johnson Street footbridge we see the imposing building and canopy over the lines. Passengers could travel to Southport for 22p (4/3d in old money). Curving away to the left are the lines for Blackburn, while those to the right are for Lostock. The three signal posts are of interest. All of them have a small calling on arm at the bottom, which allowed an engine to enter the section ahead even if it was already occupied and the other two arms were "on". In this way, vans, wagons and coaches could be added or removed from trains in the platforms by a second engine. The middle and right-hand posts have upper quadrant arms, while the left-hand post has typical L&Y small lower quadrant arms. Bolton West signalbox was the first electro-pneumatic box in the country when it opened in 1903. Instead of the traditional manual movement of wires and rods to operate signals and points, compressed air (controlled by the flick of a switch) moved machinery, and semaphore signals (later replaced by colour lights). *(Signalling Record Society: Scrimgeour Collection)*

Bolton, c1910. After the inability of the L&Y and the LNWR to amalgamate in the early 1870s, the L&Y had to put its house in order, as it had a very poor reputation with the travelling public. The main route west from Manchester was through here, and its cramped and inadequate facilities were the cause of many delays. In fact, prior to the direct line, many eastbound trains divided here, one section going to Yorkshire and the other to Manchester. The view of many passengers was that services via Manchester would take a long time and consequently the place was best avoided! So although the direct line was only three miles shorter than the original line, it (and the Wigan avoiding line) led to a transformation of the company's services and image, and relegated Bolton to a much lesser role. However, the general increase in traffic in this period meant that the station was still not up to the job, resulting in rebuilding in 1904. The area between the Trinity Street and Orlando Street bridges was cleared, and a new station built in the space. This view of the fine station buildings is along Trinity Street, the name adopted from 1896. Interestingly, it wasn't built in the two types of bricks generally associated with L&Y stations, but simply using red brick. The LNWR also had a station in the town, a terminus at Great Moor Street. A contract to renew the bridge across the lines in 1962 cost about as much as the contract to replace the whole station around the turn of the century. *(Stations UK)*

L AND Y STATION, BOLTON.

Bolton, 1964. This view north from Orlando Street bridge shows the new station layout well. It consisted of two 1116ft island platforms with four roads between them. Around the sides, there were three lines as well – a generous provision well able to cope with the services the company wanted to run from it (around 400 trains arriving and departing even before the 1904 rebuild). Illustrating the versatility and the problems of travel by train is this 25th August view. Due to their length, the main platforms could accommodate more than

one train at a time. Nearest to us on the up main platform is a service from Blackpool to Rochdale with class 5 4-6-0 No 45495 easily able to cope. To the rear is a service from Horwich to Manchester with Stanier 2-6-4T No 42654 in charge. In spite of the lack of crossovers halfway along the through lines, with sensible diagramming of trains a lot of permutations of destinations were possible. However, the platform arrangements at Victoria station sometimes dictated the departure times of trains from places such as here, so a ten minute wait was not unusual. Also note how far the front train is from the booking office. With cars being more convenient, it was not surprising that passengers sought other ways of travelling. The driver of Standard class 4 4-6-0 No 75040 in the up loop watches events before he takes his parcels train south. *(D Hampson)*

Bolton, 1963. Mention has already been made about the L&Y service to Southern Ireland. To cope with the more numerous passengers to Belfast and the Isle of Man, the company ran trains to Fleetwood. Five boats were bought and jointly operated by the L&Y and the LNWR from 1870. On 1st May 1901, the L&Y started a special service to the port, building a special 8-coach train for the service, complete with corridors and dining facilities. At that time, coaches were often separated into smoking and

non-smoking; Bolton was usually the only stop. Some years later, a train from the port arrives at platform 2 on 12th October with Vulcan-built class 5 4-6-0 No 45078 of 1935 in charge. This train, the 2.10pm from the port will have had coaches from Blackpool North attached at Poulton, and with stops at Preston, Leyland, Chorley, Bolton and Salford, Victoria would be reached in fractionally under two hours. *(Peter Hutchinson)*

Bolton Trinity Street, 1963. Looking across the through lines we witness the 12.30pm from Southport at platform 2, and as the station clock shows, it is time for departure. The train will stop at all the stations to Manchester, terminating its journey at 2.10pm. A traveller missing this train could have caught the next ordinary service from Southport, some thirty minutes later. Pausing only at Wigan and Salford they would actually arrive in Manchester about 10 minutes earlier, due to the later train (destined for Bradford) using the direct line from Wigan. *(Initial Photographics, BWL Brooksbank)*

Bolton, 1953. Waiting to depart from platform 3 on 15th August is the "Radcliffe Rocket". Heading the train will be ex-L&Y 2-4-2T No 50731, a service many people associate with such engines rather than express trains. Although on the wrong

platform, the train will soon pass across to the up main line before turning east at the junction towards Bury. It was at a meeting in Bolton on 24th January 1845 that the promoters of the Bolton, Wigan & Liverpool Railway decided to extend their proposal east to Bury and beyond to meet the Heywood branch of the Manchester & Leeds Railway. A name change to the Liverpool & Bury Railway was also approved. The next year, the new company was given leave to join with the Manchester & Leeds Railway, which in turn the following year became the L&Y. *(HC Casserley)*

Bolton, Lever Street Footbridge, 1962. The massive 1904 L&Y warehouse dominates the skyline, and has the words "London Midland and Scottish Railway Goods Warehouse" in white across the top. Adjacent to the building is Orlando Street as it crosses the railway. In 1901, the bridge was extended some 170 feet to accommodate the extra lines to the warehouse. The service, the 5.47pm from Horwich to Manchester, is hauled by Stanier 2-6-4T No 42633 on 18th August. The first vehicle, a 6-wheeler, is probably one of five stores vans that worked from the central store at Horwich to former L&Y sheds. Probably *en route* to Newton Heath, it will go to the other sheds in a circular manner before returning to Horwich. *(D Hampson)*

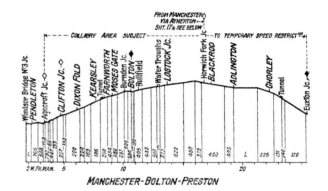

Bolton East Junction, 1964. This was the interesting view from Orlando Street bridge looking south. Across the background is the Lever Street footbridge, spanning the lines to Manchester, straight on, and to Bury and Rochdale, to the left. The controlling signalbox with its 145 levers, dates from the turn of the century (1902) enlargements in the area, as does the footbridge. Due to rationalisation, in two years time, only 95 of its levers would be needed. The train in view is the 2.30pm stopping train from Rochdale to Wigan. It can be seen after coming from behind the box and curving onto the down slow in readiness to stop at Trinity Street station behind us. *(CB Golding)*

Burnden Junction, 1962. With the time just after ten past four, the 3.55SX from Manchester is slowing down, and preparing to stop at Trinity Street station in a few hundred yards. Hauling the modest train on 13th August is Stanier 2-cylinder 4-6-2T No 42665. After Bolton the train will go to Darwen and then all stations from Blackburn to Chatburn. Oddly, many trains along this route didn't stop at Salford after leaving Victoria. *(D Hampson)*

Bolton, Burnden Junction. Looking towards Bolton station in the distance we see the line east to Rose Hill junction curving away to the right just after the line passes over a road bridge. Bolton Corporation's coal-fired power station at Back o'th'Bank was along the Astley Branch on the line to Blackburn. Complete coal trains from there were turned at this triangle of lines to and from the Wigan area until it closed in 1979/80. *(JA Sommerfield)*

Rose Hill Junction, 1959. The main Manchester Road passes under the line on the left and the line on the right. Behind us is the main line with Bolton East Junction well off to the left and Burnden Junction to the right. In the distance is the meeting of curves from the main line to make a triangle – Rose Hill Junction. On the right, replacing an earlier greyhound track, can be seen the floodlights for Burnden Park, then the home of Bolton Wanderers football club. Adjacent to that is the morning shunt from Moses Gate with Fowler 7F 0-8-0 No 49544 in charge. On the line from Rochdale is a double-headed train bound for Aintree and the Grand National meeting. Ex-LNER class B1 4-6-0 No 61305 is the train engine for the service from Hull with Ivatt 2-6-0 No 46418 acting as pilot engine. *(D Hampson)*

Passing Bolton Engine Shed, 1959. Originally opened in 1875, and enlarged in 1889, was a shed on the down side of the line south of Burnden Junction. It was coded 14 by the L&Y, and this number persisted until 1935 when the LMS made it 26C. Passing along the up main line with an express for Manchester is Hughes-Fowler "Crab" 2-6-0 No 42869 with Crescent Road shed to the left. There were many collieries in this area, for example, Burnden colliery and Great Lever colliery, both part of the Earl of Bradford's Collieries. From 1885, the Bolton Railway Wagon & Iron Works Company had been building wagons (chiefly coal wagons) on a site opposite the shed. They manufactured shell cases during World War I, later becoming Parkinson's boiler works. Another adjacent works continued repairing wagons until the end of World War II. Houses in "The Sheddings" now occupy the site. *(EV Richards)*

Bolton Engine Shed: A Study in Tanks

1954. If any engine epitomises the L&Y, it would be its "Radial", 2-4-2 tanks, one of which, No 1008, has been preserved. Officially they were "2-4-2 side tank engines", and they were the largest family of engines in England in their day, 330 engines being built between 1889 and 1911. Only Aintree shed did not get an allocation. While they are thought of as small tank engines, they were often in charge of heavy express trains over some of the most arduous of lines on the system. An inquiry in 1928 into the practise of using such engines to haul express trains showed how reliable these engines were – an average of getting on for ¾ million miles over their lives to that point. This engine is getting near pensionable age; built as No 1159 in 1892, it was withdrawn in 1956 as No 50650. *(BPC)*

1936. This design was probably the last by Hughes for the L&Y, Horwich building ten of them in 1924. It was intended to build sixty more like No 11115 here, but they were heavy on fuel and repair costs. They were replaced by the Fowler 2-6-4T of the LMS. The frames for the next twenty had already been made when the decision not to proceed was taken, so the front parts were used as frames for 4-6-0 tender engines. Consequently the last twenty of that class had a slightly longer wheelbase than the rest of the class. *(G Coltas Collection)*

1959. Fowler was the Locomotive Superintendent of the MR from 1909 until the Grouping in 1923. In the new LMS company, Hughes was preferred, but Fowler succeeded him in 1925, and brought a Midland view of things. This 1930 design was a smaller, lighter version of his highly successful 2-6-4T engine. Its classification, 3, was painted above the engine number 40015 when photographed on 4th April. Why they earned the nickname "Breadvans" is unknown. *(SV Blencowe)*

Green Lane, Bolton, 1962. Approximately half an hour after it left Horwich, the 5.47pm scurries under the bridge. Stanier 2-cylinder 2-6-4T No 42630 would have languished at Bolton for ten minutes, and will stop only at Salford and Manchester Victoria stations. There were four lines from Bolton to Moses Gate, 1¾ miles south. Crescent Road shed, on the left is causing the smoky atmosphere. *(D Hampson)*

Moses Gate, 1960. With the time approaching 8.00am, a train that started off at Rainford Junction has arrived here by way of Wigan and Bolton. After stopping here, Victoria station is almost 25 minutes and five more stops away. Stanier 2-cylinder 2-6-4T 42632 should have no difficulty keeping the four coaches to time. North of the station were extensive goods yards and sheds. In that area, the four tracks from Bolton station coalesced into two serving the platforms here. *(D Hampson)*

Moses Gate, 1965. The extensive canopies will soon be replaced by "bus-stop" shelters. With Bolton station less than two miles ahead, the driver of Britannia class 4-6-2 No 70014 *Iron Duke* will be trying to gently slow the train (probably the 16.07 for Blackpool with coaches for Barrow) ready to stop there. After Bolton, the next stop would be Preston; many LNWR services for the Lake District and Scotland ran over L&Y lines to Preston via Bolton.

Subsidence of its own track from Eccles Junction to Wigan meant that fast running was very difficult. *(D Hampson)*

Moses Gate Exterior, 1965. Tucked away just off the Bolton Road on Dover Street was this uninviting building that, apart from a notice, gives no clues to its use. Although dating from 1888 when improvements were carried out, the building isn't of the typical two-colour brick style, but is simply fit for purpose. The platforms were accessed by long covered ramps from the booking office. *(Lancashire & Yorkshire Railway Society)*

Farnworth Exterior, 1965. Opening directly onto Bridge Street was this rather unimposing entrance. Often referred to as "Tunnel Station" it became Halshaw Moor from 1845, and Farnworth was later added to the title. A reversal of names in 1870 gave the wording seen here. *(Lancashire & Yorkshire Railway Society)*

Farnworth, 1965. Looking north towards Bolton, this view shows the massive covered footbridge that connected the two sets of buildings and the platforms. This was a passenger-only station. *(Lancashire & Yorkshire Railway Society)*

Farnworth Tunnel Portals, 1966. In the top picture, we are looking south with the original 1838 tunnel on the right. However, when the MR opened its route to Scotland from Hellifield, it reasoned that there was potential for business from Manchester and surrounding area. As its loading gauge was larger than that of the L&Y, some alterations had to be made on the route via Bolton, Blackburn and Clitheroe. Here, it was decided to avoid disruption by building another bore through the obstacle rather than widening the existing tunnel. The line on the left opened in 1880. Drivers on St Peters Way (the A666) now pass over the top of the line here without even noticing, and trains race through its 295 yards without blinking. The bottom picture is from the south looking north – it is interesting to compare the different styles of brickwork. *(Lancashire & Yorkshire Railway Society)*

Kearsley 1968. The name Ringley was on the station nameboards when the line first opened in 1838. Changes via Stoneclough then Stoneclough & Kearsley were adopted before the company settled on today's name. It is interesting to note that as well as a small waiting room for Bolton bound passengers, there was a canopy over a small part of the platform, but no such facility existed on the up platform. Access was from a brick booking office on Station Road just behind the photographer. The name means "meadow of water cress", and the influence of the River Irwell is ever present. South of here, it receives much abuse, but it wasn't always so. There was an Agecroft Amateur Rowing Club in the 1860s, and the area was subject to serious flooding every few years, the obelisk in Peel Park, Salford commemorating the flood in 1866. From 1847 to 1867, horse racing was held at Castle Irwell Racecourse in Salford. After many years at Ordsall Lane, it returned here in 1902, ceasing in 1963. *(ND Mundy)*

Kearsley 1960s. The line here is down to Manchester at 1 in 186, and having raced through the station, an excursion heads south towards Salford, probably from Blackpool. One of the newer, Fairburn-altered, 2-6-4T No 42148 will have no problems with its load of eight non-corridor coaches. In the summer, anything serviceable was pressed into use, including engines. In the background, are the chimneys and cooling towers of Kearsley power station, which was built by the Lancashire Electric Power

Co in 1929 on land south of the station near the River Irwell. Colliery connections passed under the main line to take coal wagons to the power station, and wagons were hauled by electric locos fed from overhead wires. Another engine was added in 1936, and two more after World War II. At its peak, 20,000 tons of coal were consumed each week, but due to the gradients on the branch only 7 or 8 wagons could be handled at a time. The run-down started in 1969, and electricity production ceased in 1981, houses being built on the site from the early 1990s. One of the engines is preserved at the Manchester Museum of Science & Industry. *(BPC)*

Kearsley Branch, 1964. To access the Bridgewater Collieries, the company built a short double-track branch. At its junction with the main line were a series of exchange sidings with space for 224 wagons on the down side. By this time it was operated as a single line, and here "Austerity" 2-8-0 No 90419 is going up the 1 in 45 gradient towards the exchange sidings. Many pits of the Manchester Collieries Ltd contributed to its exports, including Ashton Field, Brackley, Linnyshaw and Sandhole, but the working out of the coal seams and the development of the M61 means that there is now little evidence of the branch. *(D Hampson)*

Colliery Siding, North of Clifton Junction, 1961. Having negotiated the junction at Clifton, this express train (probably for Blackpool) runs along the main line on the western bank of the River Irwell. In the background is the brick viaduct that carried the other line from the junction (the former East Lancashire Railway) over the river and along its eastern bank to Bury. Adjacent collieries at Newton and Wet Earth, along with Pilkington's Pottery & Tile Works, connected with the main line here, hence the down loop. They also joined the rival LNWR lines on their Clifton branch. Although the gradient is up at 1 in 200 all the way from Agecroft Junction to Bolton, it wouldn't challenge this engine too much, even though its appearance suggests that it wasn't being cared for very well. Jubilee class 4-6-0 No 45560 *Prince Edward Island*, one of a batch of 50 built at the North British Locomotive Company's Hyde Park works in 1934/5, would not see its thirtieth birthday. *(WD Cooper)*

Clifton Junction, c1910. Looking towards Salford, this shows the small waiting facilities on the down platform, complete with footbridge. On the left is the diverging line to Bury, built by the Manchester, Bury & Rossendale Railway in 1846. This capitalised on the omissions from the original 1838 line that only went to Bolton, even though it had Bury in its title. Passing across the picture at a lower level is the 1850 LNWR Clifton line from Patricroft on the right. After passing under the

Bolton platforms and into the "V" of the station, it will rise up to meet the Bury line at Molyneux Junction. The Wet Earth Railway connected a colliery of that name, Robin Hood sidings and Pilkington's pottery & tile works with this line here. When the L&Y electrified the line from the east end of Victoria station to Bury, it needed to generate electricity, supplying sub stations at Radcliffe and at Victoria in Manchester. A power station was built to the east of here, adjacent to Clifton Hall, the company carrying its own coal from this line in a fleet of hopper wagons. Water from the adjacent canal was used in the cooling towers from 1916 to 1933. Redundant sidings from the power station were used by the firm of Magnesium Elektron from 1937, whose by-product, chlorine, was put into tankers and stored temporarily in Pendlebury tunnel. The factory ceased to be rail connected in 1966. *(Stations UK)*

Clifton Junction, 1955. Standing on the up main line, this shows the divergence well – Bolton on the left and Bury on the right. As the gradient is up towards Bolton there are catch points on that line to derail any runaway wagons. The line to Bury became part of the East Lancs Railway later in the year it was opened, 1846. Running powers were needed from the L&Y for the 3¾ miles from here to Salford, but a conflict arose due to the L&Y feeling that they were being cheated by the ELR over the number of passengers the latter was declaring over its lines to Salford. In 1854, the section in dispute became under joint ownership, rather like the section from Walton Junction to Liverpool Exchange, but it wouldn't be until 1859 that the two companies formally amalgamated. Curiously, this 1901 signalbox has the frame facing the rear with the signalman having his back to the line when pulling the levers. *(Signalling Record Society, Scrimgeour Collection)*

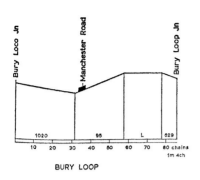

BURY LOOP

Lines To and Around Bury

With the opening of the line from Heywood to Bury on 1st May 1848, and thence to Liverpool via Bolton six months later, the L&Y had a route from Yorkshire to the docks at Liverpool independent of other railway companies. All went well until fifty years later when a west to south branch from Salford to the Manchester Ship Canal was opened. This posed a problem for trains from Yorkshire – if they travelled via Victoria station to Salford, they not only caused congestion, but they were facing the wrong way and a reversal would be necessary in both directions. To make operations easier, a short line (about a mile in length) was built to enable west to south manoeuvre to take place. A short chord was opened on the line from Heywood to the line leading to Clifton Junction, which enabled trains to approach Salford facing the right way round for entry to the Ship Canal branch.

Above: Molyneux Junction, 1956. Looking south, this view shows the L&Y line from Clifton Junction to Bury. The 1850 LNWR connection to Patricroft can be seen curving away to the right, and dropping down to a lower level. There were several collieries in the vicinity that accessed the line, and a passenger service was tried in 1853 which lasted only three months. As the main L&Y line arrives at Clifton Junction, the LNWR line has dropped sufficiently for it to pass underneath. Behind the photographer is the start of a viaduct that passes over Fletcher's Canal, the River Irwell and the Bolton, Bury & Manchester Canal. From it, the line on the western bank of the river to Bolton can be seen, including Robin Hood sidings. *(Signalling Record Society, Scrimgeour Collection)*

Bury Loco Junction, 1950s. On the left are the lines to Bury Bolton Street from Manchester. South of here, at Radcliffe North Junction, the electrified lines curve east towards Prestwich and onto Victoria station, leaving the line to Clifton Junction to go south. On the right is the loop line that bypasses central Bury. Hughes-Fowler "Crab" 2-6-0 No 42719 is waiting to proceed from the link onto the main line. In the junction created is this 48-lever L&Y signalbox dating from 1898. *(Signalling Record Society, Scrimgeour Collection)*

The loop line passed to the east of Bury engine shed. Here are a couple of representative engines that called there.

Bury Shed, 1933. Peacock 4-4-0 No 10108 would have been used on passenger turns. L&Y engine No 984 has just returned to active service after an extensive lay up, and would be withdrawn the next year. To its rear is a Barton Wright 0-6-0ST for shunting, while adjacent is 0-6-0 No 12174 used on freight trains. *(HF Wheller)*

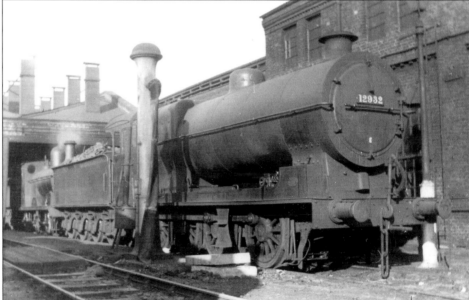

Bury Shed, 1935. Looking past the company water column into the eight-road shed, we see an example of an engine that the L&Y developed to haul its massive coal trains, 0-8-0 No 12932. Built in 1919, it wouldn't live up to Aspinall's expectations, as it only had a life span of eighteen years – he was expecting thirty. *(RK Blencowe)*

Bury Loop Junction, 1956. Looking west from Alfred Street, this shows the end of the link. In 1848, the original line from Heywood to Bury, Knowsley Road passed through the right hand arch of Heywood Street bridge. The link deviates to the left and when built, the opportunity was taken to access a pair of loops just beyond the bridge. Interestingly, the signals are hoisted high for the link and not for the main line; train speeds would have been faster on the main line, so one would have expected greater visibility. Controlling events is the 48-lever L&Y box of 1898. Vandals set fire to it on 24th March 1967, so the loop closed from that date. *(Signalling Record Society, Scrimgeour Collection)*

Meanwhile... Back on the Original Main Line via Bolton...

Agecroft Junction, 1983. Powers were granted in 1883 for a link to pass from Windsor Bridge to Agecroft on the main line to Bolton; it opened on 13th June 1887. At its southern end was a connection to Agecroft shed from 1899, and at its northern end it met the line to Bolton at Agecroft Junction. In 1902, the L&Y built a wooden, 65-lever, signalbox there. However, due to mining subsidence, it started to fall down. A replacement was built on the opposite side of the line, and opened in 1950. Looking backwards from a Bolton-bound train we see the brick

replacement. There had been colliery workings here since Andrew Knowles started in 1844, and connections to the railway and over the line to the Manchester, Bolton & Bury Canal were the outlets until the late 1920s, when the pits were abandoned. However, with around 8 million tons of workable coal still underground, a new pit was sunk to tap into the seams soon after Nationalisation. Coming on stream in 1960, the colliery was linked by a conveyor belt system to the 360MW power station across the road. Mining ceased in 1990. *(JGS Smith)*

Brindle Heath Sidings, 1976. A box consisting of a brick base and wooden cabin opened here in 1883. It is likely that it was modified in 1899, as its duties would have changed with the opening of the link between the Bolton line and the direct line. Its 42 levers controlled access to a down loop and a series of sidings called Brindle Heath Old Sidings (Low Level). In the background, to the left of the cabin, can be seen a bracket signal post and to the extreme left, a glimpse of the roof of Brindle Heath Junction signalbox. *(N D Mundy)*

Pendleton, 1966. This station was built by the Manchester, Bolton & Bury Railway and named Pendleton Bridge. With its access from Station Street, the first passengers were carried some time between the line's opening on 29th May 1838 and 1843 (according to various sources). The platform's canopies can be made out on the left, and behind them is the canal, whose owners actually promoted the development of a railway. This was in sharp contrast to the Parliamentary battles that many early railways had. *(Lancashire & Yorkshire Railway Society)*

Pendleton, 1946. A solitary member of the station staff appears to be the only witness to a stopping train from Bolton arriving at the up platform. In charge is Stanier 2-cylinder 2-6-4T No 2640 with what today would be an enormous train for such an

activity. It was renamed as Pendleton (L&Y) from 1st June 1889 to distinguish it from the younger station on the direct line. However, it was locally known as Pendleton Old, and although never listed as such in the timetable, it was sometimes referred to by this name in announcements at Victoria station. It closed on 5th December 1966. *(Stations UK)*

The Direct Line via Atherton

The thirteen miles of quadruple line between Windsor Bridge No 3 box and Crow Nest Junction opened in stages during 1887 and 1888. Bolton could be avoided by means of this line, and with the aid of the Pemberton loop, Wigan too. Its construction resulted in competitive trains between Liverpool and Manchester, and the residential trains to Southport and Blackpool vastly improved. Prior to its existence, there were few connecting services at Manchester linking towns both to its east and west. Indeed, there would have been little point in advertising such trains, so notorious was the company for poor service and delays, particularly at Manchester. The direct line was one of the components that would alter this, and unite the company's titular counties into one great railway. Receipts in 1900 were 50% more than they had been 20 years previously. Notwithstanding the general increase in trade in those years, the increase in profitability shown by the L&Y eclipsed its rivals. Sloth and indifference had been replaced by vibrancy and vision.

Crow Nest Junction, 1956. This view looking east from the adjacent road bridge shows the impact of the direct line on those that already existed. To the left of the box are four lines; the pair next to the signalbox is the original, 1848, route from Bolton. Shining and standing out alongside it is a wooden signalbox. Crow Nest Sidings box marks the joining of the up and down loops from this junction to the Bolton line. On the extreme left is the Hilton House branch dating from 1868. This joins the Bolton to Preston line at Horwich Fork Junction. Dwarfing them both in sheer scale and smoothness are the quadruple lines on the right of the box – the direct line. Thirteen miles east of here it will meet the original line at Windsor Bridge, Pendleton. As can be seen from the track layout, many kinds of exchange between lines was possible, the only one not possible was from the Hilton House branch to the down fast lines (the pair on the extreme right).
(Signalling Record Society, Scrimgeour Collection)

Dobb's Brow Junction

Railway companies often spelled placenames wrongly. The village just over a mile east of Hindley, has no "s" in its title. While the direct line allowed services to the west to be speeded up, it did little for northbound trains, but by making a 1¼-mile curve northwards from here, a link to the 1868 Hilton House line, and a further 2½ miles north to the line from Bolton to Preston at Horwich Fork Junction could be made. So, eight months after the new line to Hindley was opened, the L&Y opened this West Houghton Connection line allowing trains for the West Coast from Manchester to avoid both Bolton and Wigan, and have their first stop at Preston. This series of pictures by Wilf Cooper (some taken from the steps of the box) illustrate the junction well.

Above: Fast Lines, 1953. Looking east, we see the points and signals ready for this train to pass north, probably bound for Blackpool; it is hauled by Jubilee class 4-6-0 No 45574 *India*. The main route is the line to Hindley, hence its taller signal post. When the engine was built around 1936, it was meant to have a 4,000 gallon Stanier tender, but received the smaller 3,500 gallon variety that was destined for Royal Scot No 6115. It was well over twenty years before it received its proper tender, getting one originally destined for a Stanier 2-8-0.

Opposite page, top: On the connecting line, 1953. The 56-lever box dating from 1904 is well positioned to watch a northbound express pass through the junction obeying the 30mph speed restriction. Both up lines are blocked, and the signals for the slow line are on this lattice post with lower repeater arms. The train has just left the down main line, and is heading towards Hindley & Blackrod Junction, 1¼ miles ahead. Class 5 4-6-0 No 44934 is one of a batch of 95 engines built locally at Horwich in October 1945.

Slow Lines, 1953. A stopping train consisting of a 3-coach set of non-corridor coaches, and a rogue coach passes over the junction to follow the route set by the signals to Hindley.

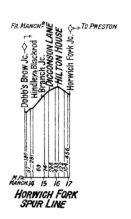

Dobb's Brow Junction, 1952. Having successfully negotiated the junction, the crew of Standard class 4-6-0 No 73026 can now increase their speed as they head towards Preston. This 3½-mile cut off was a good idea, but for footplate crews it meant extra work, as over 2½ miles of it was up a gradient at no less than 1 in 75 after a restriction on the train's speed at the junction. Trains going towards Manchester would be able to see the signals controlling their entry onto the direct line as they are easily seen above the Wigan Road bridge. Both fast and slow routes along the direct line were accessible from this connecting line.

Hindley & Blackrod Branch Junction, 1968. This was where the short connecting curve from Dobb's Brow Junction met the 1868 Hilton House Branch north from Crow Nest Junction. This branch was developed as a way of moving goods from the Chorley, Preston and Blackburn areas to Wigan and Liverpool on the L&Y's own metals rather than relying on others to whom a fee would be payable. This wooden 20-lever signalbox was photographed after the last timetabled passenger train along the line, a Blackpool to Manchester DMU, on 25th August. Due to its remote location, passing light engines brought correspondence and water cans. *(Stephen Leyland)*

Dicconson Lane & Aspull, 1951. This view looking south shows Stanier 8F 2-8-0 No 48635 from shed 16A, Nottingham. It is heading north along the up line with a light engine headcode. The station first appeared in the timetable in May 1869. A ramp leading down to the Bolton Road is at the end of the platform and a shelter sufficed for Chorley-bound passengers. Like many stations, it suffered from shortage of staff in World War I, so its activities were suspended for over two years from 2nd April 1917 to 1st May 1919, finally closing in February 1954. A Chorley to Wigan train ran into two light engines near here with one fatality. *(Stations UK)*

Dicconson Lane & Aspull, 1951. As can be seen from this view north, the station was a passenger-only affair with no goods facilities. Wigan-bound passengers had the benefit of enclosed facilities. Controlling the down line is a bracket signal with distants for the junction (Hindley & Blackrod) about a mile away. The more important route towards Crow Nest Junction is indicated by the taller post, and the lower post is for Dobb's Brow Junction. Just west of the line in the village of Aspull was the large Dicconson cotton mills. *(Stations UK)*

Hilton House, 1949. Looking south from the road bridge, reasonable provision for passengers is evident. Access was by ramps from the bridge with large notices reminding passengers to use these to cross the line. Note the clock on the Wigan platform to inform the greater number of passengers travelling that direction. The wooden 24-lever box and tall signals date from 1916, and were built to control access to the nearby Scott Lane colliery. The up connection was just under the bridge we are on, and the down was beyond the platform on the right hand side. *(Stations UK)*

Hilton House, 1959. Opening with the line in May 1869, it closed in February 1954, and like the other station on this line, the L&Y suspended its services in World War I. This view from the Chorley platform has the Manchester Road bridge with the Hilton Arms Hotel on it. Just under the bridge on the left was a line to Scot Lane colliery, which opened in the late 1850s and relied upon the Aspull pumping station of the Wigan Coal & Iron Co for drainage. However, its successor, Wigan Coal Corporation decided to shut down the pumps, and all the pits were drowned, closing in August 1932. *(Stations UK)*

Horwich Fork Junction, 1963. This was the meeting place of the original line from Bolton to Preston and the branch from Crow Nest Junction with the chord from Dobb's Brow Junction. The line from Bolton is on the left with its bracket signal clearly visible above the nearby Red Moss footbridge. This was the position of the original junction of the line from Crow Nest, but in 1889, the junction moved north to here. The curve, behind us, from south to east and taking a line to Horwich, dates from 20th June 1887. This view, looking south from Ridgway bridge carrying Moss Lane over the line, captures a Manchester to Blackpool train pulled by Jubilee class 4-6-0 No 45591 *Udaipur* on 5th July. It has just come from Dobb's Brow Junction and as the signals show through the smoke, will take the main line to Chorley. *(D Hampson)*

Blackrod Station, 1960. Having laboured up the line from Dobb's Brow Junction, the engine is now running down the gentle gradient towards Euxton Junction. Given the presence of Station Road bridge, it will have burst into the station, much to the delight of the young trainspotter. Hauling a train destined for Blackpool from Manchester is Jubilee class 4-6-0 No 45653 *Barham* on 8th July. The station probably opened with the line from Bolton towards Preston, but has had several identity crises regarding its name, starting as Horwich & Blackrod. The branch from the north of the station was opened to Horwich on 15th July 1868, and it became Horwich Junction two years later. However, Blackrod appeared in the name again three years after that, with Horwich disappearing from 1888. The signals are for the junction ahead along the up line – Horwich Fork. The yellow distant arms were left for Bolton and right for Wigan. *(D Hampson)*

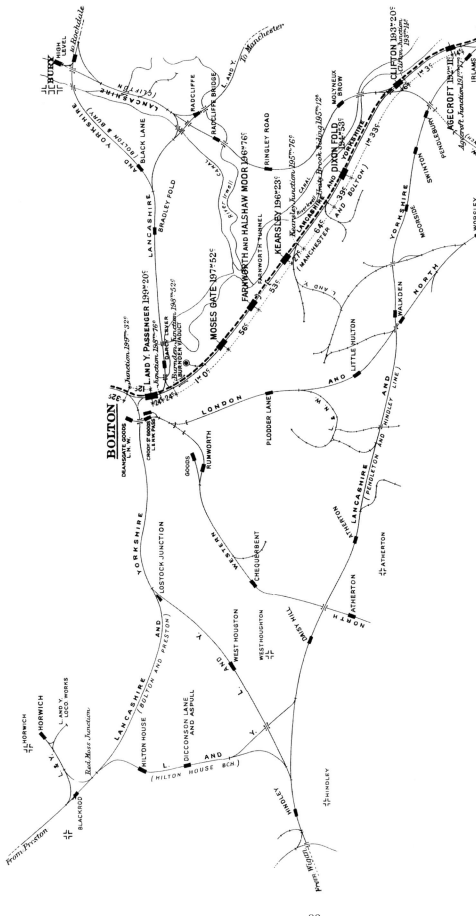

The lines in the area are nicely shown on the Midland Railway Distance Diagrams.

WIGAN (L. & Y.) ..dep	8 40	8 55		1055			0 4 25	1	5 40	8 0		9 30		3 30 7 30
Ince ... "	6 45	9 0		1055			5 4 30		5 48	8 5		9 34		3 34 7 34
Hindley ... "	6 50	9 4		11 0			1 10 4 35		5 52	8 10		9 38		3 38 7 35
Dicconson Lane. ... "	6 54	9 8		11 4			14 4 39		5 55	8 14		9 43		3 43 7 43
Hilton House ... "	6 57	9 12		11 7			17 4 42		5 55	8 17		9 46		3 46 7 46
Horwich Junction ... "	7 0	9 16		1111			21 4 46		5 59	8 21		9 f 1		3 51 7 51
Adlington ... "	7 5	9 20		1115			25 4 51		6 3	8 25		9 56		3 58 7 56
CHORLEY ...... arr	7 12	9 27	10 9	1123	1252		33 5 0	5 14	6 10	6 14 8 34	9 10	10 3	10 6	4 3 8 16

Extract from the 1873 timetable, showing that Blackrod station was then called Horwich Junction.

89

Blackrod Station, 1964. A single platform with a wooden shelter was built for the Horwich branch with access via this footbridge connecting the northern end of the main line platforms. A short distance along the branch was a curve from the Bolton direction, opened on 20th June 1887, and creating a triangle. Trains could therefore leave Horwich and travel to Bolton via Fork Junction or go to Blackrod station for connections with main line trains. *(Lancashire & Yorkshire Railway Society)*

Blackrod, 1947. A group of friends interrogates the fireman in No 10617, and I bet one of the questions was, "Mister, can we have a ride in your engine?" Sidings north of the station were used to organise wagons for the short line to serve Cooke & Nuttalls paper mill at The Vale Works, "Pug" No 11249 having been sold to the firm in 1936. Due to the success of this type of train, two more complete units were built at Horwich in December 1911 (L&Y 16 and 17). Six more were ordered in 1914, but the order was cancelled. *(BPC)*

Horwich Station, 1947. Opening on 14th February 1870 this station caused the one at the junction to split its name. Shuttling between here and Blackrod (with some going to Bolton) was a railmotor service using a small tank engine with a coach, the end of which was adapted for the driver to sit in. By means of communication wires, he could inform the fireman (still in the engine) what to do. To start with, both engine and coach had the same number, but as they were maintained separately, this pairing was dropped. Shedded at Bolton (26C) is 0-4-0T No 10617 with trailer No 3. On the left is what looks like a second trailer that could be added in peak times. As the load became too much for the engine, standard tank engines with one or two coaches were used. Next year, this unit was withdrawn, outlasting its fellows by well over ten years. *(HC Casserley)*

Horwich Works. In May 1884 the L&Y bought 650 acres of Lancashire countryside close to its main line from Bolton to Preston, as the existing works at Miles Platting and Bury were deemed inadequate for the job of revitalising the fortunes of the company. The Locomotive Superintendent of the company had been Barton Wright since 1876. Supported by J Ramsbottom, he laid the foundations of a modern works using experience gained from Crewe, Derby and Swindon. From 1886, Aspinall built on this to create a works that made a lot of what was needed to build, repair and run a railway. These views of the erecting shop show some of the arrangements for the 30-ton overhead cranes (Horwich had twenty) that made jobs so much easier, and that were lacking at their former premises. The way of working was for a team of men to strip and rebuild several engines at a time. In 1932 (right) a 4-4-0 engine is in front of a radial tank body. Sister radial tank engine No 1008 was the first engine

built here in
February 1889. In
1959 (above) we
see 0-6-0 No 11304
(a converted tank
engine) on jacks
with the "new"
thinking behind it –
an engine with all
its working parts on
the outside of the
frames to minimise
maintenance. Some
of the most famous
engineering names
had streets in
Horwich named
after them, for
example,
Ramsbottom,
Fairburn, Naysmith
and Whitworth.
(WL Good & BPC)

Back on the Direct Line...

Daisy Hill, 1952. An express train, probably from Aintree races, has left Dobb's Brow Junction a mile behind, and is putting up a good show of steam as it passes east along the up fast line. LNER B1 class 4-6-0 No 61040 *Roedeer* is in charge. Partially obscured by smoke is the typical two-colour brick booking office at street level. The chimneys for the platform buildings are of a similar construction. *(WD Cooper)*

Daisy Hill, 1951. A good picture of gents' toilet provision by the L&Y! This view is west along the down, Liverpool, platform that opened on 1st October 1888 with the line from Atherton to Hindley. Only the part of the canopy by the steps down from the road bridge being maintained. There were only passenger facilities here; a Manchester-bound train is on the down slow platform. On 11th May 1987, a station was opened south of here at Hag Fold, with platforms either side of the lines. *(Stations UK)*

Atherton Central, 1950. This fine view west shows the station as it was opened by the L&Y on 1st July 1888. This and Pendleton Broad Street were the only two stations on the direct line with platforms serving the fast line on the left. The booking office on the main road overbridge and the covered footbridge serving the platforms are typical features. Built for the opening of the line is this 16-lever wooden signalbox. On the right is a bay platform for services to Manchester, access being from the down slow line. Just under the footbridge was the goods yard accessed from the slow lines. Laburnum Mill is the imposing building to the rear. *(Stations UK)*

Opposite page bottom: Atherton Central Exterior, 1965. A station was opened by the LNWR in 1831 as Bag Lane, becoming Atherton by 1847. On its arrival, the L&Y station needed a suffix, so Central was adopted until 1965, by which time Bag Lane had been closed for 11 years, so the suffix was no longer necessary. The typical L&Y building on Upton Road housed a booking office and an area to store parcels, and had access to the bridge to the platforms as well as a small canopy for the protection of passengers from the weather. *(RJ Essery Collection)*

East of Atherton, 1952. Crewe-built Jubilee class 4-6-0 No 45719 *Glorious*, dating from 1936, scurries along the down fast line with a westbound service; it would continue doing this work until March 1963. As the gradient is slightly down here, and speeds of 75mph were common, restrictions due to mining subsidence were in place in many locations from Rainford Colliery to Pendleton. While the signals controlling its progress are mostly hidden by the telegraph post, those for its fellow travellers in the same direction, and that for the up slow show up well. As is evident from the accompanying spoil tips, there were several collieries with connections to both the L&Y and the LNWR lines. Peelwood was worked from 1882 to 1928 with Peel Hall Sidings further east. A line from New Lester colliery, burrowed under the L&Y line making a connection with a line from Peel Hall colliery. Although the colliery closed in 1943, a new coal washing plant on the site of the former Peel Hall colliery dealt with coal from opencast workings. *(WD Cooper)*

Ellesmere sidings, 1959. South of the line were the lines of the Bridgewater colliery, while north was Ellesmere colliery, and complicating matters, the LNWR line from Eccles to Wigan. Both colliery lines had access to both main lines – Walkden sidings on the LNWR and Ellesmere sidings on the L&Y. The wagons on the right are on the tracks from Walkden sidings, while the track cutting across the picture curves behind the engine and up to the sidings with the wagons in the background (Ellesmere sidings). The main L&Y line passes over this site by the bridge on the left (note the nicely curved brickwork) which, a few hundred yards to the east, passes over the LNWR line adjacent to Walkden (Low Level) station. The main lines had speed restrictions imposed due to subsidence. The engine, *Kenneth* was built for the North Staffordshire Railway at Stoke in 1921, and was allocated No 22, later becoming LMS No 2264. It was bought to work colliery lines in 1936, which it did until it was withdrawn in 1961. Many of the pits here owe their existence to Francis, 3rd Duke of Bridgewater (also called "The Canal Duke"). He inherited the title in 1748, and set about expanding the business. Ellesmere colliery was worked out after 60 years in 1920, and then became a pumping station until 1968. It wasn't a large undertaking, employing only 114 underground workers and 32 at the surface in 1896. Walkden Yard (see map) was the main workshop for the Bridgewater Colliery Railway from 1900, and become the central workshops for No1 (Manchester) Area of the National Coal Board. The name lives on as the Ellesmere Shopping Centre in Walkden. *(Photo: BPC, 1929 Ordnance Survey map reproduced by permission of the Ordnance Survey)*

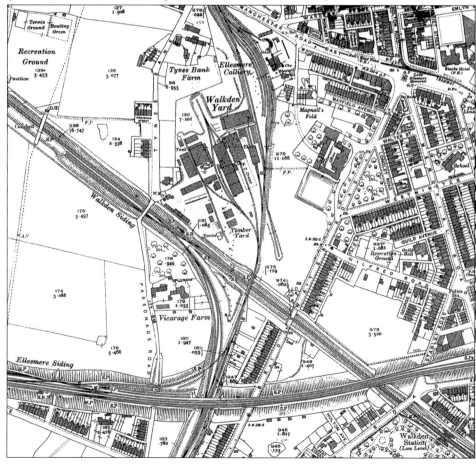

Walkden, Exterior, 1966. Even though the station was sandwiched between the slow lines, the company still used the familiar bricks and patterns to advertise its presence, austere as it was. On the left is the girder bridge for the up slow line, while the right-hand bridge carries its partner as well as the pair of fast lines. *(Lancashire & Yorkshire Railway Society)*

Walkden High Level, 1950. Opened as plain Walkden by the L&Y on 1st July 1888, High Level was added by the LMS on 2nd June 1924, as it then became responsible for the L&Y rival's station (the LNWR had a Low Level station on its line from Eccles to Wigan, also known as "The Stocks", with its entrance from Brindley Street). While the L&Y station had around twenty trains each way each day taking about 23 minutes to go to Victoria, the LNWR had only five a day taking five minutes longer, and there were none between 10.00am and 4.00pm. Not surprisingly, the nearby Low Level station was closed in 1954. *(Stations UK)*

Walkden High Level, 1950. The same figure watches an express on its journey to Liverpool. Note the standard buildings on the gas-lit platforms. As the country emerged from the effects of the war, repairs to canopies such as this were low on the priorities. With shades of "1984", rumour has it that the local town hall clock was made to strike thirteen at the desire of the Duke of Bridgewater, as coal workers were returning late after their meal break saying they hadn't heard the clock strike one! *(Stations UK)*

Walkden High Level. It is rather obvious why these engines became known as "High Flyers", as one tears past the station with one of the celebrated "Forty Minute Express" in L&Y days. Even though the line between Liverpool and Manchester was more steeply graded and longer than its rivals, trains such as this, lightly loaded with few coaches could keep to time; Victoria station is ahead. The engine is one of the 4-4-2 Atlantics developed by Aspinall in an attempt to improve the image of the L&Y. Two batches of twenty of these engines were built in 1899

and 1902. Note the lamps on the front of the engine, and there are two brackets by the chimney – the idea of putting both lamps just above the buffers to denote an express passenger train wasn't universally adopted until the start of the 20th century. *(BPC)*

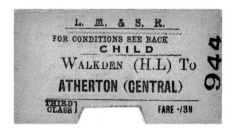

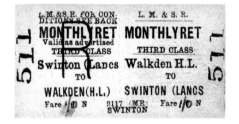

Walkden, Date Unknown. This is one of Aspinall's celebrated "Radial" tank engines. Several sister engines, with short bunkers, were adapted for use in "reversible trains" as the L&Y quaintly called them. The first such service was along this line in 1922 between Manchester and Atherton, making the return trip seven times a day. This particular engine, No 10923, was built at Horwich as No 267 in November 1898. Improvements included a Belpaire firebox in May 1911 and a Schmidt superheater in April 1914. It belonged to class 5 according to the L&Y, and only 4-4-2 Atlantics and the Hughes 4-6-0 were rated higher. It was withdrawn at the end of the LMS era in November 1947, so never carried a BR number. *(WD Cooper)*

Walkden Troughs, c1960. There are few flat sections on the line, and here a shallow cutting and embankment were needed to provide a stretch long enough for troughs, whose inflows were heated in cold weather. Class 5 4-6-0 No 45017 heads an express west on the down fast. Supplying the troughs was a large storage and treatment tank to the right from which a pipe ran to the troughs, with a ballcock arrangement cutting off the supply when the troughs were full. The troughs were approx 18in wide and 6in deep, the scoop on the tender dipping into the top half of the water only. To pick up water an engine's speed needed to be above about 25mph, and in about 30 seconds, between 2,000 and 3,000 gallons could be taken on board. Being too slow winding up the scoop meant that passengers in the front compartments had a watery surprise, as here! *(WD Cooper)*

Moorside & Wardley, 1956. Having just raced through the station, the 6.10pm from Manchester Victoria is heading towards Wigan, on its way to Southport. Class 5 4-6-0 No 44736 and its very clean coaches will stop only at Meols Cop and St. Luke's in the suburbs of Southport before arriving at Chapel Street in fractionally over an hour. The equivalent train in 2006 was the 17.38, stopping at six more stations, and taking a few minutes longer. Partially obscured by the smoke are the signals for the up lines, lifted high for sighting purposes due to the presence of bridges and pipes, one of which (the Thirlmere aqueduct) carries water from the Lake District to Manchester. *(BKB Green)*

Above: Moorside & Wardley, 1946. The signals for the down fast stand out well above Moorside Road, 1½ miles east of Walkden. The facilities on the island platform, serving the slow lines only, are similar to those at Swinton and Pendlebury. This section was opened by the L&Y on 1st July 1888; BR shortened the name by dropping the second part from 6th May 1974. *(Stations UK)*

Left: Moorside & Wardley, 1963. Looking towards Liverpool. The small goods yard, complete with a crane that could lift up to 5 tons, is on the left, and was accessed from the slow lines by trailing crossovers controlled by the 32-lever box, which closed in 1968. *(D Hampson)*

Moorside & Wardley, Entrance, 1965. Straight off of the main road was this small booking office in the distinctive L&Y style. *(RJ Essery)*

Near Moorside, 1946. An unidentified 0-6-0 goods engine, the most numerous type on the L&Y, heads along the slow lines towards Manchester. It is interesting to note how the loads on the wagons are positioned so that they won't make contact when going round sharp bends. The company had extensive timber yards at the docks in Liverpool. With today's passenger dominated railway, it is difficult to believe that until the late 1960s, railways earned more revenue from freight than from passengers. *(WD Cooper)*

Near Moorside, 1905. Heading along the down slow line is a stopping train hauled by 4-4-0 No 979. Dating from the start of Aspinall's era (1888) they were not wholly of his design. Faced with an acute shortage of engines capable of hauling the increasing number of express trains, he ordered a batch of 20 from Beyer Peacock to the basic design of Barton Wright with 6ft driving wheels; they were probably delivered in green livery. This "Peacock" was later allocated to Blackpool, and could be taking this interesting collection of coaches "home". Later it became No 10103, lasting until 1932. *(TE Kite)*

Swinton, Exterior, 1966. The typical L&Y entrance abuts directly onto Station Road, and here the building is slightly bigger than its neighbours. Forty years ago, a day return to Blackpool cost 14/6d, (73p), today it costs £11.70p. Adjacent to the station was the home of Swinton Rugby League Club. *(Lancashire & Yorkshire Railway Society)*

Swinton, 1946. The looks very much like a clone of Pendlebury, with the station entrance being where Station Road crossed the four tracks. The station opened with this section of the line on 13th June 1887, and it is still open. Between the two bridges are the sidings of Swinton Goods Yard, complete with its 10-ton crane – one of the biggest on the line. *(Stations UK)*

Swinton, 1972. By now, the two fast lines have been removed, and the signal controlling the down line has been moved. It is good to see the extensive roof still intact and in good repair, rather than having been removed as is so often the case. The brick booking office and steps down to the platform can be seen on the bridge. *(JA Sommerfield)*

Pendlebury, 1939. Next to the road bridge was a 201-yard tunnel, to the east of which the station was opened on 13th June 1887; access was by the footbridge from the Bolton Road. Looking west, the booking office is on the left, as are the fast lines, with the slow lines having a platform and canopies. The signals have white backboards to make them stand out. The station closed 3rd October 1960. *(Stations UK)*

Pendlebury, 1962. At nearly 4.40pm, the 3.18pm ex-Southport leaves the station for Manchester; serving all stations apart from Meols Cop. Today's trains take around 20 minutes less, but the connections at Wigan to Bury and Rochdale no longer exist. Class 5 4-6-0 No 44689 makes light work of the few coaches, as it passes the 32-lever box dating from the line's opening. The L&Y signal for the slow line contrasts with the BR signals cantilevered over the up fast. Fast to slow transfers were possible, hence the other arm on the bracket . The box closed in 1966, six months after the fast lines. *(D Hampson)*

Pendlebury. Bursting under the Cliveley Road bridge is a westbound express with Jubilee class 4-6-0 No 45652 *Hawke* in charge, and directly underneath the position of the first coach is the tunnel that carried the LNWR Clifton branch. This engine was one of a batch of 48 built at Crewe. Starting life in 1935, it lasted thirty years. *(WD Cooper)*

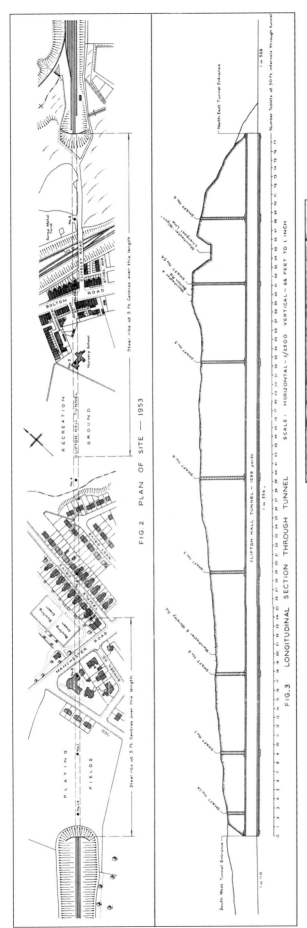

FIG 2 PLAN OF SITE — 1953

FIG.3 LONGITUDINAL SECTION THROUGH TUNNEL

SCALE : HORIZONTAL — 1/2500   VERTICAL — 66 FEET TO 1 INCH

CLIFTON HALL TUNNEL — 1299 yards

Clifton Branch of the LNWR

Tunnel entrance. To access collieries in the area, and to show its intent (to stake a claim for the area over other interested companies, as the railway politics of the day dictated) the company built this short line from its own metals at Patricroft, north east, to meet the L&Y at Molyneux Junction, along the line from Clifton Junction to Bury. The line had to pass through the higher ground around Pendlebury by means of a tunnel, some 50 to 60 feet below the surface. Allegedly, the foreman of builders had big black whiskers hence the tunnel being called "Black Harry tunnel".

Tunnel diagram. The line here was straight, and the 1,299-yard tunnel was brick lined with eight shafts used during construction; it opened on 2nd February 1850. Later, steel bracing was put on the tunnel lining from both ends as a precaution against subsidence from colliery workings. The line wasn't a great addition to the rail network, but a limited passenger service was tried for three months in 1853. From 1909-10 Pendlebury expanded and houses were built on top of the ground that the tunnel went through. Apart from occasional summer excursions from the Rochdale area to North Wales, its limited value can be gleaned from the 1951 working timetable, which showed three northbound and one southbound mineral train a day. On 28th April 1953 at 5.35am, a police inspector living in Temple Drive observed that two houses "just disintegrated into the ground", killing five people as they did so. The inquiry into the deaths showed that numbers 22 and 24 and the end of number 26 Temple Drive were built directly above shaft No 3, which had been covered over at tunnel level with timber. Over time the shaft had become filled up, and the wood had rotted, leaving the brick tunnel lining holding up the weight of the sand and rock above it. When the wood ceased to offer any help, the bricks gave way, depositing into the tunnel the accumulated earth above, and with it, the houses that were built on top. Prior to the accident, an inspection had revealed some bricks on the line, so traffic (such as it was) was stopped and steel rails ordered to counteract the collapse. Temple Drive now has a gap in its houses.
(BR Accident Report, picture – Salford Local History Library)

Pendlebury Bank, 1962. East of Pendlebury, the pair of fast lines rises up and passes over the slow lines, at Brindle Heath. They then descend to be north of the slow lines at Pendleton, thus allowing the slow lines to access the goods yards at Salford (and later, the Manchester Ship Canal) without conflicting continuously with the passenger trains on the fast lines. Jubilee class 4-6-0 No 45607 *Valiant* comes down the gradient on the down fast line, and is about to pass the station. The train is probably one of the fastest from Manchester to Southport, the 4.10pm. With stops only at Wigan and St Luke's, the 35½-mile journey would only take 58 minutes. In fact, with a connection at Chapel Street, even the "posh" suburb of Birkdale was within an hour of Manchester. The double junction the engine is passing over allows up-fast to up-slow and down-slow to down-fast transfers. *(D Hampson)*

Pendlebury Bank, 1957. Coming down Pendlebury bank is an express on the down fast line passing a stopping train on the down slow, which is preparing to stop at the station. The express hauled by class 5 4-6-0 No 44765 will tear through the station. Not only did the direct line fulfil the objective of allowing L&Y to compete with other companies for the Liverpool to Manchester service, it also allowed the Manchester to Wigan, Southport and Preston service to be accelerated as well. *(WD Cooper)*

Irlams o'th'Height, 1910. With the growth to the east of Manchester, a "minimal" station was opened by the L&Y on 1st July 1901. Costing £6,783, it consisted of a single timber island platform on the slow lines, just beyond the carriage sidings. There were two buildings, the smaller one in the background housing a porter's room and a gents' toilet at its far end. Canopies were provided on both sides of the larger building, and inside was a booking office with a general and ladies' waiting room. The method of platform construction, the canopies and the nameboard lettering all show up well in this view taken not long after opening. A lane, later called Bank Lane, was built over during the construction of the line, and provided an access route later

when the station was built. This made it handy for the adjacent carriage sidings at Irlam and Agecroft engine shed. This area was the starting point for the East Lancs Road, planned in the 1920s, but actually opened by King George V in 1934. With parallels to the original railways, it bypassed Warrington, Wigan and St. Helens.
(Stations UK)

Irlams o'th'Height, 1951. Like most railways, the L&Y lost a large number of employees as volunteers when World War I started. By early 1915, 4,189 had enlisted, causing real problems for the smooth operation of the railway, so in 1917, the company appointed its first Station Mistress here, and indeed, the complete station staff here was female. By the end of the war, around 4,400 females were employed on the L&Y, but 3,300 of them would have their employment terminated when the

men on active service were demobbed. There was no equality in the world of work at that time. The hipped roofs have been replaced by flat canopies. The fast lines (or "top lines") are to the extreme left of the picture, slowly reducing their elevation until they are the same at Pendlebury. The station closed on the 5th March 1956.
(Stations UK)

Brindle Heath Junction, 1961. At this point, the slow lines pass under the fast lines. Arriving from the north is a connecting line from the original route via Bolton, and the line from Bolton joins with the slow lines from Liverpool here. To avoid conflict with the fast lines from Liverpool, the latter were taken up on an embankment and over the converging slow lines to come down to the north of them. The western ends of the slow line's loops were controlled by Brindle Heath Junction box's 100 levers. Looking north, we see the access to the extensive up sidings, with a capacity of over 800 wagons. Agecroft locomotive depot is between Agecroft Generating Station and the box, and the 60-coach carriage sidings branch from the down line to the left. The up coal train, hauled by "Austerity" 2-8-0 No 90292, has passed Agecroft colliery, and is signalled to pass along the up slow line towards Manchester. *(WD Cooper)*

Brindle Heath, 1962.
Passing along the down slow line is a stopping train for Wigan hauled by Fairburn 2-6-4T No 42180 on 23rd April. The engine is passing over the pointwork for the separation of the line to Bolton, the tall signals to the right indicating which route the driver is to take. The fast lines, above the engine, have risen up, and are now passing over this junction and the slow lines. By this means, unhindered running was achieved, and the fast lines were in the best position for the route towards Wigan. Just in front of this train are the carriage sidings at Irlam, and on the right are Brindle Heath down sidings. *(WD Cooper)*

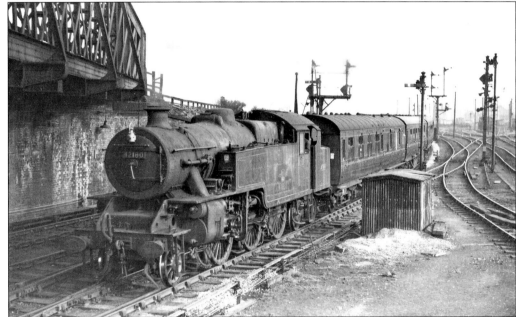

Brindle Heath Down Sidings, 1976. This small, 20-lever box opened in 1899, and controlled the sidings south of the slow lines. *(ND Mundy)*

Agecroft shed, 1934. This 8-road shed (No 13) on the connecting line between Brindle Heath and Agecroft Junctions opened around 1900. Of around 100 engines, about 80% were for freight duties. To the side of the shed is the main line to Bolton and Brindle Heath up sidings with large numbers of wagons in them. The engines that called at or were based here range from 2-6-0s and 0-6-0s to 0-8-0s and 2-4-2T engines. On the right is the shed foreman's office with company water columns standing like sentries. *(A Appleton)*

Agecroft shed, 1950. A scheme to improve locomotive depots on the LMS commenced in 1933. Called, "Motive Power Area Locomotive Power Supply, Repair, Concentration and Garage Scheme", it cost over £1million and brought best practice from here and the USA to over fifty depots. In 1937, coaling and ash plants were erected at Agecroft, the original coal hole surviving as a water tank. A wagon is being hoisted up the side of the concrete coaling tower for its contents to be tipped into one of two 75-ton capacity hoppers. Engines are performing all the steps in the sequence: coaling, ash disposal, watering and turning. *(WD Cooper)*

Agecroft Shed, Date Unknown. "High Flyer" 4-4-2 No 1423 poses in the shed yard. If this picture was taken in 1908, it was allocated to Low Moor shed. Built in 1902, it survived until 1927, being withdrawn as LMS No 10338. The well-known writer on L&Y matters, Eric Mason, was shed foreman here around the Grouping. To improve efficiency, Aspinall adopted the use of punched cards developed in the USA by Herman Hollerith (whose company, with others, was later to become IBM). Using this system, it was calculated in 1913 that each passenger engine earned £1,825 per annum and each mineral or goods engine earned £2,290 per annum. In the background is the Agecroft emergency breakdown train, consisting of a tool van, a travelling van, a safety wagon (No 3150) and a 10-ton hand crane (No 1197). There were similar trains at Bury, Bolton and Wigan. *(AG Ellis)*

Agecroft Shed, 1926. For shunting heavy loads, the L&Y developed a 0-8-2T version of its 0-8-0 tender engine. There were other minor variations such as oval buffers and a wheel to secure the smokebox door, in addition to slightly larger cylinders and both middle pairs of drivers having wider, flangeless treads. Although popular with engine crews, the 1908 design was not repeated. This pair is testing the newly installed 70ft turntable here, which replaced a 50ft one. On the left is No 1504, which spent most of its life here after a brief spell at Aintree, where it evicted the engine on the right, No 1505, to Accrington as a spare engine. Returning here preceded its demise the next year, two years before its sister was withdrawn. *(BPC)*

Agecroft Shed, 1920s. Although this class was built in the LMS era from 1926, the design was L&Y with compromises for the LNWR and MR lines they would have to traverse. Hughes was the CME of the L&Y before the Grouping (from 1904) and of the new company afterwards, but he had resigned before Horwich works built the design he encouraged, Fowler (another ex-L&Y man) being in the top job at that time (although he made no significant contribution to the design). Interestingly, the MR 3,500 gallon tender was adopted. According to the 1945 allocation, 21 of this type of engine were shedded here. *(BPC)*

Agecroft Shed, 1920s. Although undated, the condition of No 10448 suggest it has been newly constructed at Horwich in June 1923, complete with LMS crest on the cabside. It was allocated L&Y number 1677, but never carried it. Given the operating requirements of the newly-formed company, many members of this batch of the last 20 engines (including this one) spent most of their time between Crewe and Carlisle. As new LMS engines were built, some returned to their intended lines hauling heavy seasonal trains in the summer months. *(BPC)*

Agecroft Sidings, 1973. A coal-fired power station was first built by Salford Corporation in 1924, close to the banks of the River Irwell. Further power stations were added in 1950 and 1962, and all were partially fed with coal from the adjacent colliery by means of a conveyor belt over the railway lines. However, this colliery couldn't meet their demands, so coal was brought in from others, typically by the modern motive power seen in the background. To handle the wagons in the CEGB sidings, a team of (ultimately) three Robert Stephenson & Hawthorns 0-4-0ST locomotives were ordered. Two were delivered in 1948, and here we see the second, named *Agecroft No 2*; the third arrived via Back o'th'Bank power station in Bolton in 1954. Their services were dispensed with from 1981, all three engines being preserved (this one is at Preston after a spell at Southport Steam Centre). The power stations were all closed by 1993, the skyline being restored to its original appearance the next year. *(G Coltas)*

Irlam, 1914. Deputising for the regular 4-4-2 or 4-6-0 engine is 2-4-2T No 746 on Saturday 30th May. The train is the 1.15pm from Manchester to Southport and Birkdale, ascending the bank on the fast lines. In pre-electric light days, gas-lit wooden coaches with fires in the locomotives hauling them were a fire risk, and two accidents on the MR prompted railway companies to look for ways to avoid such disasters. The L&Y built "fireproof" coaches, whose outside panels were of steel, with floors protected on the underside with fireproof material, and gas reservoirs provided with automatic shut-off valves to prevent gas escaping. Should it ever become necessary, emergency windows were fitted near the centre of each coach to allow rapid evacuation of passengers. This rake of carriages illustrates well the company slogan "The Business Line", adopted from the turn of the century. On weekdays its workings would be from Southport's stations, resulting in a "race" of well under the hour; businessmen could return home at the same pace. This meant that the stock made a 74-mile return trip every day, but languished without earning any revenue from 9.00am to 5.00pm. *(E Mason)*

Irlam, 1963. Having recently departed from Pendleton (Broad Street) one can almost hear the engine puffing and wheezing up the gradient as this stopping train heads north-west along the down slow line. To the left of the engine are the fast lines coming down the gradient, which will soon be at the same level. The train is passing over a viaduct across several streets, for example, Laundry, Villiers and Railway Streets, having just passed a magnificent bracket signal. The two smaller arms on the right

indicate two down goods loops that access Brindle Heath down sidings; the eastern ends of the loop are on the right. Just in front of the train between the fast and slow lines was Irlam signalbox. Engine No 42180 is one of Fairburn's modifications to the 2-6-4T design introduced during his brief time as CME of the LMS from 1944-5. *(WD Cooper)*

Irlam, 1962. This was the place where the two pairs of lines came next to each other. The slow lines are to the right of the picture, and shortly the fast lines will rise at a gradient of 1 in 99, slackening to 1 in 132 for the next two miles, to allow them to pass over the slow lines at Brindle Heath. A gantry for the up lines with its metal arms shows up well. The signalman in Irlam's box has pulled lever no 34 to move the top arm on the left-hand post to the off position. To the train about to pass along the left-hand line (the up fast) it will signify that it should slow down and be prepared to stop at the next home signal. This express is on the down fast line with class 5 4-6-0 No 45326 in charge. Built in 1937 as one of a batch of 227 engines from the works of Armstrong-Whitworth, this engine lasted until 1962. *(WD Cooper)*

Pendleton Broad Street, 1962. With Manchester Victoria 2½ miles behind it, this express is just getting into its stride. Having glided round the curve through Broad Street station, it will have to tackle a gradient until Swinton is reached, another 2½ miles distant. Some carriages carried roofboards saying "Manchester-Southport". The train is heading west on the down fast line, while its partner is to the left and is signalled for a train to sweep through the station. Visible through the bridge is the up face of the island platform serving the slow lines. There are two pairs of signals for that direction, as east of the station is an opportunity to transfer to the fast line. Engine No 44731 was one of the almost last batch of locomotives of this class, being built in 1949. Costing £11,826 each, they were well over twice the price of fellow class-mates from 1935. I wonder what its scrap value was in April 1966! *(WD Cooper)*

Pendleton Broad Street, 1974. Broughton Road, Pendleton crosses two sets of railway lines. The first was built by the progenitor of the L&Y, the Manchester, Bolton & Bury Railway, whose station, with its access from Station Street, was named

Pendleton Bridge on its opening some time after the line was opened from 29th May 1838, but before 1843. The second set of lines, arriving some 45 years later, served the direct line. As both stations were operated by the same company, some method of distinguishing between them for passengers was necessary. The new station was actually called Pendleton New until July 1896, before becoming Broad Street, even though that street is around 100 yards south. Having been closed for many years due to a fire, the buildings were finally demolished here in August 2003. George Bradshaw, of timetable fame, was born at Pendleton in 1801. *(G Coltas)*

Pendleton Broad Street, 1946. This view northwest is of the newer station with its short, 44-yard tunnel under Ford Lane and Broughton Road. The section from Windsor Bridge to Swinton was the first to open on 13th June 1887, and the provision for passengers reflected the anticipated level of service and patronage. Only this station and Atherton had four platforms, the other six stations having platforms only on the slow lines, the whole route being quadruple and laid out for fast running. Since 1824, a horse bus service to The Exchange in Manchester had been in operation, at 6d a journey, many times throughout the day. The area was fast becoming an expensive residential district for those who wanted to

escape from Manchester (Salford did not come into being until 1844) to their large houses in, for example, Leaf Square. The railway company reasoned that such customers needed to be theirs. The two lines seen here are the up slow (left) and the down fast, the up fast is on the extreme right around the island platform. By this time, most trains stopped at the slow lines platform only judging by the canopy. The booking office at road level has steps leading down to both island platforms. Note the down fast signals on the wrong side of the line, due to the curve, and the white backboard, to aid sighting. *(Stations UK)*

Pendleton Signalbox, 1966. The photographer was standing at the Manchester end of the island platform that served the pair of slow lines. This brick-based box was built for the opening of the line in 1887, and was modified by the L&Y in 1899, probably for something like the insertion of the crossover. The main use of its 28 levers was as a block post, and to control a double junction that allowed down trains to pass between the fast and slow lines at 25mph. Cantilevered out for greater visibility over the up slow lines are the BR replacement signals; the main route is the tallest post (up slow). Both these posts and that for the up fast on the left, have two arms on them. While the top red-painted home arms are operated by this signalbox, the lower, yellow-painted distant arms are worked by the box in front, Windsor Bridge No 3 some ⅓ mile south. In the background to the left of the box are the signals for the down direction. There, the main route is the fast line, so its post is the tallest. *(BPC)*

Windsor Bridge No 2 Signalbox, 1956. Looking towards Bolton we see Windsor Bridge; today's Salford Crescent station (opened 11th May 1987) is just the other side of this bridge. Using the LNWR, the Manchester South Junction & Altrincham from Castlefield Junction, and the L&Y here, a route now exists that connects the two largely-separate railway systems in Manchester. A station opened here with the line as Pendleton, Windsor Bridge, but closed in June 1856. The 50-lever box signalled only the goods lines and a bi-directional goods loop from No 3 box. An 1887 building was replaced by this one in readiness for the opening of the dock lines, some four years later. After the Manchester Ship Canal was opened, a double track line went down to New Barns Junction to meet the MSC lines at Salford docks.

Windsor Bridge No 2 Signalbox, 1956. This view is towards Manchester with the signalbox adapted to fit the situation and its footbridge connecting with Albion Street. The extensive sidings curve away to the left to serve a large coal yard and on the right, the cattle station. Above the main lines on the left was a wagon repair workshop. Diving down at 1 in 47 in a brick-lined cutting are the lines to the docks, the bracket signal controlling their entrance to the goods lines. On the left in the distance are the three gables of the former Hope Street engine shed. This 6-road facility boasted a 50ft turntable, and operated from 1871 to the opening of Agecroft shed in 1889.
(Both: Signalling Record Society, Scrimgeour Collection)

Left: Windsor Bridge No 3 Signalbox. Almost half a century after the first railways were built in this area, the peace was shattered again when the direct line from Hindley met the original line to Bolton. Controlling events is the 50-lever box in the top right, opened in 1898. On the left is a fine bracket signal controlling the oldest lines, the taller post indicating the most used route, the fast lines through Salford and east to Victoria station. The other two arms control the slow lines east, and on the right is a pair that indicate transfer to the up goods and the control of Windsor Bridge No 2 box. Passing along the down slow, probably on its way to Agecroft shed, is class 5 4-6-0 No 44818. The signalman has pulled lever No 33 to raise the top arm; the bottom arm is operated by the box in front, Pendleton Broad Street. Judging by the other signals controlling the down lines, a fast train is about to pass this way. The direct line's up fast signals give a choice of routes on the way to Victoria. The other arms on that bracket are for the up slow line. Goods trains from the docks would simmer on the line to the extreme right awaiting their slot in-between stopping passenger trains on the down slow of the direct line. *(EF Bentley)*

Windsor Bridge Cattle Station, Date Unknown. Although a poor quality photograph, it is included to give an insight into the L&Y in its early days. In the early 1900s, Salford livestock market was the most important in the north of England. Opening on 7th November 1885, Windsor Bridge cattle station cost £8,559. The LNWR had its Cross Lane cattle station only a stone's throw away across Liverpool Road. The neatly organised sidings and cattle pens, complete with lights, are being shunted by an unidentifiable 0-6-0 engine, and one of Salford's gas holders is to the left in the background. The L&Y company reports contain many entries illustrating why it was held in less than great esteem by the public.

From 1859, there were regular reports concerning the carriage of passengers in excursion trains at Whit Week – they used cattle wagons! The Board was notified that in 1866 the process of using such wagons was more expensive than before, "owing to the measures to guard against the cattle plague", but the company did respond to the adverse criticism in the press, as the next year they simply made efforts to remove the white-wash as completely as possible. It took until 1873, when the company had sufficient carriages, before this method of treating the public changed. To give an idea of the volume of the trade, 96,659 live animals were imported through the MSC in 1900. *(Lancashire & Yorkshire Railway Society)*

Hope Street Coaling Stage, 1969. Even though Windsor Bridge shed was superseded by the opening of Agecroft shed, some basic equipment for servicing was retained. Coal would have been shovelled from wagons onto the wooden stage, and thence to the tender of an engine. A water column enabled locomotive tanks to be replenished, and by these means, engines could serve for days at a time without needing to go to a shed. Originally, in March/April 1908, one and later two of the Hughes 0-8-2T engines were allocated to Agecroft shed to haul trains up from the Ship Canal to the sidings here. They were reliable, and needed little apart from routine maintenance, lasting until between 1926 and 1929. The extensive lattice bridge connected Hope Street to Albion Street, while the gas holders belong to Salford's Liverpool Road gas works. *(Manchester Locomotive Society, H Bowtell)*

Ship Canal Branch c1960s. The L&Y always sought new opportunities for extra business. Even before the Manchester Ship Canal opened, the company had obtained powers in 1890 to build a short (just over one mile long) double track branch from Windsor Bridge to a site between No 8 dock and the racecourse at New Barns. Much of the £116,275 contract was used in the demolition of 177 properties, and building tunnels by the cut-and-cover method. The depth varied between 17ft and 23ft beneath the surface. This shows the first of three tunnels, here under West Egerton Street, which was the longest at 471 yards during which it passes under LNWR lines from Ordsall Lane to Cross Lane. The third line, on the left, went to a brickworks, but was later taken over by Salford gas works (visible behind). *(G Harrop)*

Ship Canal Branch, 1963. This view is looking north from the 172yd tunnel under West Park Street where it ran under a cinema on Stock Street. To the rear is New Barns Junction and the meeting with the Ship Canal railway. In the distance is the 291yd Ellesmere Street tunnel with bridges for Melbourne, Granville and Lynton Streets in between. Note the recesses for workmen to shelter in when trains passed by. After 30 months construction, the line opened on 28th March 1898, closing on 15th June 1963. The company was a little slow about getting this venture off the ground, as they had construction powers well before the 1st January 1894 opening of the canal, but didn't let the contract for the branch until September of the following year. The L&Y had to pay tolls for up to 200 wagons a day to its rivals, the LNWR, for three years until its branch was ready. To coincide with the development of the branch, the company built an equally short curve in Bury to allow trains from Yorkshire to pass straight into the docks without having to reverse. *(J Marshall)*

New Barns Sidings, 1956.
LMS 0-8-0 No 49555 sorts out its train by the seven-storey warehouse for No 8 dock facing the gridiron. It was built in this style to appease the owners of Castle Irwell racecourse, which occupied the land before No 9 dock was built. With the racecourse closing in 1867, racing was re-established in Manchester (actually Salford!) with the opening of the New Barnes track in 1876. In 1898, plans were submitted to open a 188yd platform for race traffic at the end of Race Street. It was reported to the L&Y

Board on 30th March of that year that, "platforms *(note plural)* for passenger station on Ship Canal Branch had already been put in by the contractor". Was it due to poor reporting or a lack of interest that only one platform was ever built? It was short lived, as the racecourse ceased operating in 1901, and the branch never developed any regular customers. It reopened in 1904 as New Barnes (more commonly as "The Docks") for local workers and annual children's excursions, the last recorded one being in 1939. *(Rex Conway)*

Manchester Ship Canal Railways, 1955. King Edward VII opened No 9 dock in 1905, and a large tract of land was left between it and the No 8 dock (to the left). Two large sets of loops were built on this land, one for the Ship Canal railway and one for the L&Y. Between the two gridirons, the canal company built Nine Dock Locomotive Shed, a two-road, straight shed, open at both ends. The canal company operated the largest private railway system in the UK. Once owning 75 locomotives and 230 miles of track, it gave employment to 790 people. On the left is one of its

SALFORD DOCK BRANCH

many engines bought from Hudswell Clarke of Leeds. It is one of that maker's Canal class, of which 32 were eventually bought. This example *Monti Video*, later No 40, came in 1906 (nameplates were carried inside the cabs). Several of its sisters are in view, and hiding away is a saddle tank engine. The grain elevator at the head of No 9 dock opened in 1922. *(BPC)*

Manchester Ship Canal Railways, 1960s. As railways had been firmly established as "number one" in the transport business for decades, it must have been quite a culture shock to those businessmen invited to discuss the building of old technology by Daniel Adamson in the late 1880s. However, the punitive rates set by Liverpool Docks and the railways were the spur to its development and success. A wide variety of cargo was handled by the docks, but by far the largest in volume was coal. Ships not only exported coal but consumed it themselves, so there was a steady stream of wagons just to refuel them. MSC 0-6-0T No 62 *St. Petersburg* is organising the wagons in preparation for their unloading (known as "setting the quay"). It belongs to the Hudswell Clarke Sweden class, arriving in 1914. The only real difference between it and the Canal class is that here the water capacity was enlarged from 580 to 840 gallons by bigger tanks in the front. The L&Y had a warehouse across the canal in Trafford Park Estate, with wagons gaining access from the Ship Canal system via a single-line swing bridge (doubled during 1943). *(SV Blencowe)*

Salford Docks, 1920s. While this picture was probably taken on its rival's territory, it is included to illustrate the type of cargo that ships carried along the Ship Canal – it wasn't all coal and grain. These 2-8-2 engines are destined for the metre-gauge Assam Bengal Railway, having been built by the world-famous locomotive constructor being publicised on the crane. *(BPC)*

Back on the Main Line...

Oldfield Road No 2.
Sweeping south under Oldfield Road bridge from their coalescence at Windsor Bridge are the seven lines that continue east to Salford, behind us. Controlling the up and down goods loops, as well as the up and down goods lines, is the brick-based signalbox of 1889 vintage, extended to 100 levers in 1899. Under its control are a series of loops leading north to Hope Street box, some sidings to the south, and most importantly of all,

the pair of lines that leads down to Salford goods yard. *(JA Peden)*

And off it Again...

Irwell Street Branch, 1962. A goods yard had been in existence since the early days of railways in the City. With the construction of the link from Ordsall Lane to Victoria station in 1844, and the Manchester, Bolton & Bury Canal, a triangular section of land existed at a lower level than the railways. In the early days, wagons were lifted up and down to the main lines by wagon hoists, and a report in the local newspaper in 1849 commented on the pair of towers that housed them. Movement of wagons would have been by horses with wagon turntables a-plenty. Some of the viaduct arches were used for warehouse purposes, while others were used to stable horses; in 1900 two more were converted to accommodate 29 horses. An incline from Oldfield Road down to the goods yard was authorised in 1865 at a cost of £4,180. Looking out of the back as an engine traverses the 1 in 27 to the goods yard, this view gives an indication of the steepness of the incline. Instructions were that only

one train of no more than 35 wagons could go down at a time, and sometimes they were allowed to roll down to the lower level as long as there were sufficient men to control the brakes. Illustrating the hazardous nature of work on the railways is a minute of the 1868 Board meeting, which states, "Iron handles to be fitted to goods brakes using the incline at Salford for the men who are obliged to ride open wagons to hold on by". The cost was 2 shillings (10p) per van.
(A Haynes Collection)

Irwell Street Goods Yard, 1960s. On the left can be seen the incline down from Oldfield Road. Shunting into the earliest part of the complex, "The Field", is Barton Wright 0-6-0ST class 23. The yard expanded through the LNWR viaduct into what became known as "Preston Yard". There (below) sister engine, No 51413, waits between tasks on 27th February. In the background is

the L&Y main line with the canopies for Salford station visible. As well as the engines pictured here, other types of engine that worked the yard were a Kitson 0-4-0ST, and in the latter days, a 0-6-0 diesel shunter. *(RS Greenwood & A Appleton)*

Crossing Irwell Street, 1962. The extension across Irwell Street was made possible by the relocation of New Bailey prison to Strangeways in the late 1860s and early 1870s, with the L&Y buying up the land, and naming it their New Bailey Yard. A parallel exists in Liverpool, where the relocation of its gaol allowed the development of a site near Great Howard Street station. Originally, the L&Y wanted to close off Irwell Street, but although the local authority wouldn't agree to the stopping up of a public highway, it did allow four sets of lines to be laid across it. When giving the original permission to cross the road, the Inspector stated, "The laying down of tramways worked by horses across this street between the goods station and the site of the New Bailey prison would not, in my opinion, materially interfere with its use as such an alternative route when occasionally required, especially if the use be limited, as I conceive it might be, to specific hours of the day." As can be seen here, it needed employees with red flags to control the sparse road traffic. LMS 0-6-0T No 47579 is proceeding across Irwell Street on 24th March. *(G Harrop)*

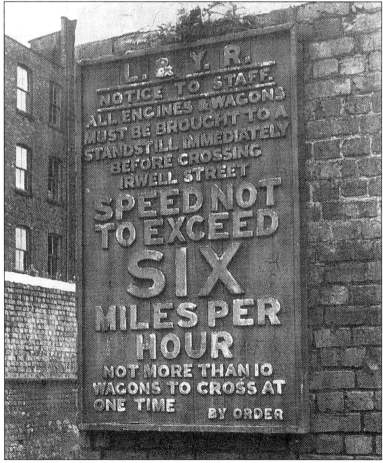

New Bailey Yard, 1962. Enemy action and record cold made 1940 the goods yard's *annus horribilis*. The air raids of 22nd December destroyed the goods shed in New Bailey Yard together with 40 wagons and two of the LNWR lines on the viaduct to Exchange station. On 3rd October of the same year, an "oil bomb" had set fire to a warehouse with cloth, rags and paper in it – needless to say, it was burnt to the ground. The shed in the background is a post-war replacement for that mentioned earlier. Illustrating why such engines were invaluable in places where tight curves abound is "Pug" No 51207. Built in December 1893, it carried the number 504. Renumbering under the LMS made it No 11207 until it received its BR number in September 1950. In great abundance are Scammell mechanical horses, 3-wheel driving units and detachable trailers that were used for the collection and delivery of goods. *(R Greenwood)*

Irwell Street Coaling Stage, 1961. Servicing the engines that shunted these yards was the responsibility of Agecroft shed. However, to avoid the occupation of the line by light engine movements, and to be more economical with their time, the company built a wooden coaling stage adjacent to the viaduct. L&Y "Pug" 0-4-0ST No 51207 and LMS 0-6-0T No 47678 occupy that space in this view. "Salford continuous engines" would spend a week in the yard starting on Monday morning at around 1.15am (in 1940) and returning to Agecroft shed, "in convoy" on Saturday evening at around 7.30 to 8.00pm. This facility was located in Preston Yard with the viaduct in the background carrying the LNWR lines from Exchange to Ordsall Lane. A view of this yard from those lines can be seen in *Liverpool & Manchester 1: LNWR Lines. (IG Holt)*

Back on the Main Line (Again!)

Salford Station, Exterior, 1966. The city of Salford is to the west of the River Irwell with Manchester being on the opposite bank. Opened on 29ᵗʰ May 1838 was the Manchester, Bolton & Bury Canal & Railway Company. Bridges were expensive, tolls had to be paid and vested interests worked hard to keep new developments in their place, so it is not surprising that the company actually never penetrated the first named city, never went to Bury and terminated at New Bailey Street in Salford. It did go to Bolton, though. At street level in New Bailey Street, there were booking offices and steps to enable passengers to get to the trains.

Lines connected the west end of the station onto the Liverpool & Manchester lines of the LNWR, which meant that trains to Victoria couldn't call here without a reversal. However, trains from Bolton could access Victoria station from 1844. The L&Y lines from Salford to Victoria only opened in 1865, and until then most of their trains terminated here. The entrance to Salford's passenger-only station was north of the 1865 bridge. With the widening of the lines in the mid 1890s, another bridge was built, resulting in the entrance being sandwiched between the two – note the less florid style of the later cast iron columns. During 2007, a major redevelopment scheme is set to transform the station as part of Chapel Street. It was in this street in 1908 that John Noel Nichols developed his herbal drink, Vimto. *(Lancashire & Yorkshire Railway Society)*

Salford, 1922. The Benn & Cronin Train Indicator was much better than the usual paper timetables, which were too easy to obliterate or deface. Departure times for all the major stations were displayed, although "Stations to Bolton" meant that you had to know along which line you were to travel; there was a lower panel for Sunday services. The date is significant – the Railways Act of 1921, which grouped the railways into the "Big Four", wouldn't take effect until the next year, but the L&Y and the LNWR took the plunge in 1922, becoming amalgamated under the LNWR banner. They had discussed such a manoeuvre before, and meetings in 1905 resulted in them agreeing to interchange tickets and the rationalisation of freight collection and deliveries in shared areas. Earlier, in 1872, they also conducted negotiations with a view to amalgamation, and in the following year, a Bill was presented before Parliament. L&Y shareholders, who were to receive an 8⅜% dividend in 1872, thought that they would get a good deal for their shares, the LNWR shares only yielding 7%, but both this Bill and the one in 1874 were thrown out, Parliament wanting competition not a monopoly situation. *(BPC)*

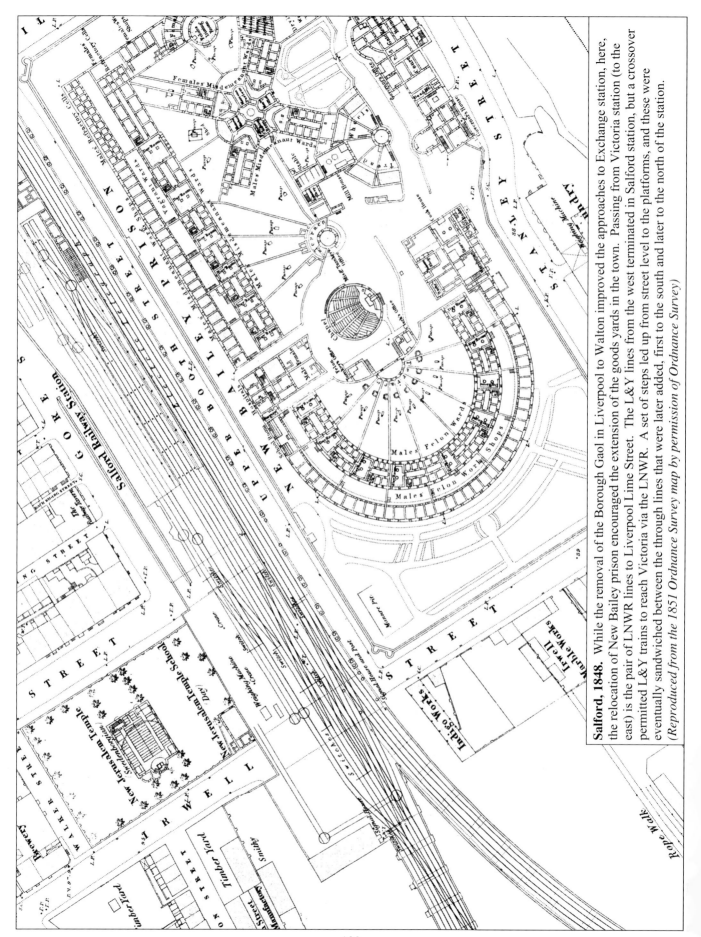

Salford, 1848. While the removal of the Borough Gaol in Liverpool to Walton improved the approaches to Exchange station, here, the relocation of New Bailey prison encouraged the extension of the goods yards in the town. Passing from Victoria station (to the east) is the pair of LNWR lines to Liverpool Lime Street. The L&Y lines from the west terminated in Salford station, but a crossover permitted L&Y trains to reach Victoria via the LNWR. A set of steps led up from street level to the platforms, and these were eventually sandwiched between the through lines that were later added, first to the south and later to the north of the station. *(Reproduced from the 1851 Ordnance Survey map by permission of Ordnance Survey)*

Salford, 1961. The original (1844) lines to Victoria from the west were built by the LNWR from Ordsall Lane, and didn't serve Salford station at all. Renamed Salford New Bailey Street in April 1858, and reverting to plain Salford in August 1865, the station, seen here on 28th April, had the suffix "Central" added on 3rd October 1988 to differentiate it from the newly opened (11th May 1987) "Crescent" station. *(HC Casserley)*

Salford, 1972. This view is looking east along the through platforms, which were created in 1865. To the left is the second set of through lines, dating from almost thirty years later, and these, together with a southern bay, gave five platform faces altogether. The widening from Salford to Windsor Bridge cost £85,255, and involved the demolition of about 100 homes in addition to the complete reconstruction of the Manchester, Bolton & Bury Canal below a new retaining wall. Salford used to be a ticket platform for all trains except the 40-minute expresses. From Salford station there ran a pair of goods lines to the south and a goods loop to the north, and illustrating the volume and complexity of railways served by just the L&Y in the area, there were seven lines for a mile to the west. *(JA Sommerfield)*

Salford, 1961. Looking west from the up fast platform, we see an express about to enter the station on 28th April. In charge is Jubilee class 4-6-0 No 45705 *Seahorse*, probably slowing down and preparing to stop at Victoria, ¾ mile ahead. On the extreme left of the signalbox is a bay platform for services that terminated or originated here. The fine bracket signal is for the down fast line, and ahead are some carriage sidings that could be accessed from here (hence the lowest signal). Railway planners did not seem to be sure where this

station was. It appeared on displays as "Salford Manchester", perhaps picking up on a description of them as "the greatest double-barrelled city in the world". *(HC Casserley)*

Salford, Looking East, 1959. Racing through on the down fast line is a businessmen's train for Hellifield, where it would meet the Midland Railway. Stanier 2-cylinder 2-6-4T No 42472 with its taper boiler should have no difficulty performing the task it was designed for – fast suburban passenger trains. Its first stop will be Bolton, followed by Darwen and then Blackburn. For the second half of the journey, every station on the line (except Newsolme) will receive a visit. Although slip coaches are most often thought of as being a GWR peculiarity, the L&Y also had some. Trains from Manchester for Blackpool slipped coaches at Kirkham, while one from Salford to Colne slipped a coach at Accrington – quite a feat as the station there was on a curve. *(BWL Brooksbank)*

East of Salford, Date Unknown. Coming towards us on the down slow line is an express from Victoria station, just over 500 yards behind it. An unidentified Hughes 4-6-0 is in charge, and it is most likely to move over to the nearest line (the down fast) by the crossover just in front of it. The first two vehicles are interesting, and are possibly luggage vans for the boat train to Fleetwood. Meanwhile, waiting to go the other way is a 2-4-2T with a rake of 3rd class suburban coaches, probably waiting for a platform in Victoria station. This train is obeying the magnificent bracket signal controlled by Deal Street signalbox, just visible above the coaches of the express. On the right is the formidable gantry of signals facing a driver on the LNWR approaches to Exchange station. *(RK Blencowe)*

Deal Street Signalbox. When the lines were widened between Salford and Victoria in 1894, the viaducts carrying the line were extended northwards. This 80-lever box was built on a widened section of the viaduct. *(Lancashire & Yorkshire Railway Society)*

Deal Street, 1920s. Heading east, having probably just set off from platform 12 at Victoria station, is a train on the down slow line as it passes Irwell Bridge sidings. Ahead, when it passes Deal Street box, it will pass to the northern pair of lines, the fast lines. The train shed for Exchange station is above the engine, 4-4-2 No 1422. This is one of the second series with the Atlantic wheel arrangement, being built at Horwich in June 1902. Having spent all of its life first at Low Moor, and latterly at Newton Heath, it was withdrawn in 1930 as LMS No 10332. The coaches, which appear to be of North Eastern design, have nameboards on their sides, and are possibly in a train from York for Liverpool. Above the coaches is a bracket signal with different facing arms. Controlling the top arm would be Deal Street box. In case you're wondering, the man on the right is of normal height – this is why these engines earned the nickname "High Flyers". *(BPC)*

Deal Street Signalbox, 1953. Standard class 5 4-6-0 No 73023 brings a mixed collection of coaches past the end of the adjacent station, Manchester Exchange (actually situated in Salford, as it is west of the River Irwell). A 4-4-0 lurks at the rear as the banker for trains needing a push up Miles Platting bank. One of the complexities that railway companies put upon themselves was in the designation of their routes. Lines to Manchester were termed "up" and those away, "down". So a train from Liverpool to Leeds would travel along the up fast to Manchester, but the down fast east of Victoria. From 1922, the former LNWR and L&Y both became part of the LMS. With the 1929 resignalling scheme, the two company's lines were connected here by double junctions in both directions, and a new Deal Street signalbox was built between the ex-L&Y northern pair of lines. The vertical and circular format of the colour lights shows up well. *(N Preedy Archive, T Lewis)*

Victoria West Junction Signalbox Exterior, 1975. By 1903, due to the sheer volume of traffic, there was a need for seven signalboxes in the area. In 1929, a new system was introduced. Remodelling of the junctions serving the station enabled a greater range of train movements between the two sets of lines from the former companies, now both part of the LMS empire. This involved abolishing six signalboxes and replacing them with two all-electric ones to control the electrically operated points and colour lights. One of the boxes, the new West Junction, was set at right angles to the running lines. All four sides were glazed to offer all-round vision, and it had a flat top. *(ND Mundy)*

Victoria West Junction Signalbox Interior, 1957. Inside Victoria West Junction box, miniature leavers operate the points and signals, and it was only in 1993 that it was replaced – testimony to good design or to penny pinching? The box communicated with East Junction 400 yards away to the east, still with its mechanical semaphore signals, and with the other all-electric box at Deal Street 500 yards to the west. *(Signalling Record Society, Scrimgeour Collection)*

Irwell Bridge Sidings Signalbox, 1972. Irwell Bridge Junction signalbox was a massive 120-lever box that was swept aside in the 1929 resignalling scheme. In it, there were two 60-lever frames that the signalmen worked back-to-back. Thus, the box could be fitted into a shorter space than if a single 120-lever frame had been used. Not to be confused with it is this 15-lever box replacing a ground frame with almost twice as many levers. Situated between the pairs of fast (to the north) and slow lines from Victoria at the west end, its main function was to control access to two loops and engine sidings, as well as a 50ft turntable between the main lines. *(JA Sommerfield)*

Manchester's Victoria Station

While there are many books and articles about this important station, the perspective here relates to the services to Liverpool as much as possible. The station was a compromise of sites in the heady railway days of the mid-1840s. With the Liverpool & Manchester Railway firmly camped in Liverpool Road to the west, and the Manchester & Leeds Railway at Oldham Road to the east, a meeting of their metals to allow cross-Pennine access to the Irish Sea ports was inevitable. Their extensions to Victoria station opened on 1st January 1844, the L&Y being the last to arrive. The two previous stations enjoyed long and fruitful lives as goods stations for over 120 further years.

The two companies created a single platform, with arrangements for both companies to terminate trains and have their own staff, as well as booking offices and entrances. The then-recently-opened station at Derby had a similar arrangement to accommodate different companies. Thus the restrictions for the future were set – the station, being between the banks of the River Irwell to the west and the smaller River Irk in the east.

In 1865, the L&Y extended its lines from Salford through the station to meet its own down from Miles Platting. Bay platforms were built to the south together with a second platform to serve the through lines. The germ was sown for the Victoria we know today.

Future building simply enlarged these facilities to produce a station that at its zenith had 17 platforms – arguably the biggest outside London. At the start of the 20th century there were almost a thousand passenger train movements a day here and at the adjacent Exchange station, not forgetting light engine movements, empty stock and freight trains that made the whole area a complex, important and exciting place.

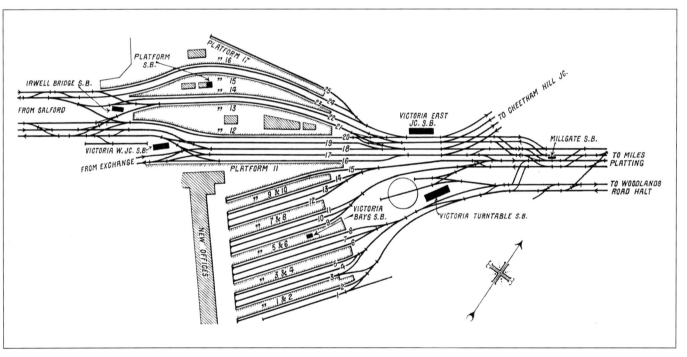

Victoria Station Track Plan, 1928. Showing up well are the two large island platforms and the cluster of terminal suburban platforms. This plan is dated a year before the LMS alterations that produced the long platform 11 in association with platform 3 of the adjacent Exchange station.

Through Lines.
Victoria station was really a station of two halves. To the north were the through lines for trains to Liverpool in the west and Leeds in the east, and to the south were the suburban terminal lines providing services to Rochdale, Oldham and the electrified lines to Bury. In between was a pair of lines that allowed freight trains to bypass the platforms, and also permitted LNWR trains to leave Exchange station and proceed east without blocking any of the

L&Y platforms. A third line, known as "Wallside" often held banking engines to assist eastbound trains, such as Aspinall 0-6-0 Nos 52094 and 52207, seen here. *(RS Carpenter)*

Travelling East, c1960. Heading an express train up to the Miles Platting bank is class 5 4-6-0 No 45339. It is most likely to be for Leeds City by way of Stalybridge and Huddersfield. Fortunately, the smoke does not obscures the company bracket signal, blackened by decades of smoke. Note the numbers of schoolboys watching this train, and their dress code! *(BWL Brooksbank)*

Travelling West, 1961. Keeping a strict watch on their speed as they descend the bank would be the crew of LNER class O4/3 No 63686. This is one of a class of 38 ROD (Railway Operating Division) engines dating from World War I. It is probably a train of empty wagons being taken back to the Ordsall Lane (LNWR) from Dewsnap sidings. It will achieve this by passing through Victoria on the through lines, and then passing between the platforms at Exchange station. *(BWL Brooksbank)*

Ex-L&Y Lines, 1952. Having descended the bank, the driver of LNER class B1 4-6-0 No 61313 carefully negotiates a path across the through lines that lead to Exchange station, and onto the through lines heading to the L&Y side of Victoria station. The train is a football excursion bound for Bolton from Nottingham on 31st January. Half-way along platform 11 on the right, is the pointwork that allows access to these through lines too. Not all descents were as fortunate. On the first day of 1936, 0-8-0 No 12771 heading a mixed freight train, descended Miles Platting bank too fast, and collided with three non-corridor coaches in platform 14 that passengers were just starting to board. The nine passengers must have had quite a shock when the runaway hit them at a speed estimated to be 60mph, and pushed the coaches 300 yards to the west – luckily without any casualties. *(BWL Brooksbank)*

Manchester Victoria, Date Unknown. Here is a double-headed train setting off west, probably for Liverpool from platform 11. The arrangement of the tracks was such that L&Y trains like these had to cross the two LNWR through lines to access their own metals; there was no access to the LNWR lines from this platform yet. Immediately in front of us is a small bay in which engines would be marshalled ready to change arrivals from the east. At this time, probably in the pre-Grouping era, there is a train shed over the through platforms. The roof over the section between the

two halves of the station was reduced in 1934/5, and further removed by Hitler in 1940, never to be replaced. I have not been able to find any examples of trains that stopped at both Victoria and Exchange stations. *(CM & JM Bentley)*

The Longest Platform in the World. From 1922, the LNWR and the L&Y were amalgamated as one company, and a year later they became part of the LMS. As a result, two platforms were to be linked – one at Exchange and the other at Victoria (platform 11) to give one platform, 2,194ft long. It wasn't a simple matter, as new junctions between the two former company's lines were needed, as well the removal of LNWR bay platforms and L&Y sidings. The bridge over Great Ducie Street was widened, and that over the River Irk (completely culverted by now) required massive new ironwork. The LMS was severely criticised for failing to look after workers' safety when three men were killed on 17th May 1925 on this work. A protective screen was built together with a canopy over this connecting platform (as a youth, I always thought this screen was built by killjoy railway officials to prevent me from being able to observe trains at the west end of Victoria!) A scissors crossover enabled trains from the middle platform to move over to the down through line at Exchange. Thus, at the same time, three trains could occupy these platforms and could depart within quick succession, so increasing the stations' capacity. Seen passing along the through lines is a freight train hauled by Class 8F 2-8-0 No 48263. *(BWL Brooksbank)*

Middle, 1967. This view is east along "platform 11 middle", and the viewer is unknowingly standing above the River Irwell. With due ceremony, this section was opened by "Railway Queen" (the "Miss British Railways" of her day) Edna Best in April 1929. This part of the platform was bidirectional enabling trains to arrive and leave from either direction. This train is the 5.45pm to Preston. According to the 1951 timetable, that would be its first stop on its way to Blackpool and Fleetwood, nicely illustrating the potential of the direct line, and how it played a part in the revival of the image of the L&Y. *(HC Casserley)*

Exchange, 1955. In the background is a double headed express at "middle" on the scissors crossover. The front engine looks like a Patriot, and the train is likely to be one from Leeds. The practice of using two engines to cope with the heavy trains over the Pennines was frequently used by the ex-LNWR side of the LMS – Patriot class engines were rare on the LMS Central division. In front of the engine is the footbridge to enable passengers to walk from the station circulating area to the island platform (numbers 4 and 5). Illustrated well by this picture is the operational flexibility that the long platform offered. If the train had stopped

a little further back, it could have passed by platform 3 or gone onto the through line. From the latter, trains could bypass Victoria altogether, and come onto Exchange's platform 3 for the waiting passengers. As a youngster I always found the instruction inside the lavatory, "Please adjust dress before leaving" amusing. *(Stations UK)*

Victoria Panorama, 1958. The time is just after 5.30pm, and the west end of the station is busy in this view from platform 16. On the left is the 5.45pm stopping train for Bolton with class 5 4-6-0 No 45234 in charge. At the other face of the island platform is the 5.40pm fast to Bolton, then stations to Hellifield; 2-6-4T No 42545 will haul that train. Meanwhile, on the other (larger) island platform, Standard class 4 4-6-0 No 75015 is ready to depart with the 5.40pm for Wigan and Southport. The other face of this island platform, No 13, was used for eastbound trains. It wasn't until the 1865 extension to here from the then terminus station at Salford that through platforms were built. Not long afterwards, in 1883, enlargements of the station created these two island platforms, which were initially numbers 6 and 7, and later became 12/13 and 14/15 respectively after the 1903 alterations. Since its inception, Victoria station has had a history of continual enlargement. *(CA Appleton)*

Entrance to Platforms, Early 1920s. As the northern part of the station was separate from the concourse and the rest of the station, the company decided to "close" the station for tickets from 3rd March 1913. This was an attempt to restrict the activities of the debris of society that are attracted to such places, and to control passengers. The suburban bay platforms had folding steel barriers since their opening in 1904, and the position of the ticket collectors was such that they didn't hinder the flow of passengers, but could collect tickets as passengers filed past. The "contracts" referred to would be season tickets in today's language. Such was the demand for Blackpool trains that only passengers for a specific train (printed on their ticket) could enter the platforms. *(BPC)*

Manchester Victoria, c1960. Arriving at the west end of the second island platform is a train from Colne, which would have arrived here by way of Blackburn and Bolton. Motive power comes from Stanier 2-6-4T No 42648 as pilot and a class 5 4-6-0 as the train engine. Its destination is Euston, which would be achieved by heading east to Droylesden, and then south to arrive at Stockport and the LNWR line to the capital. Note the extension to platform 14/15 made of sleepers and the offices on the adjacent platform. *(J Davenport)*

Manchester Victoria, 1922. Standing to the west of platform 11 is "Newton" class 2-4-0 No 731, soon to be renumbered as No 10000 – note the company crest on the wheel splasher. In 1873, the L&Y locomotive works at Miles Platting was badly damaged by fire so disrupting the flow of new builds. Outside contractors were recruited to supply engines, and this engine,

one of a batch of ten, was from the LNWR workshops at Crewe. They were well received by the L&Y, but the transaction so alarmed the private engine builders that they obtained injunctions to force the railway companies to build locomotives themselves or purchase from them. The original tender has been replaced by a combination coal and water bunker, and a Saloon, which ran on two ordinary coach bogies, placed very close together. Stationed at Horwich it was well used by Hughes when he was CME. *(BPC)*

Manchester Victoria, LMS days. In the late 1880s, the company was short of engines, so to effect delivery as soon as possible, the work was commissioned to Beyer Peacock. Thirty were delivered over seven months starting in July 1888. Originally No 996, it became LMS No 10119, and would last until June 1930, having been on the duplicate list since 1922. With 6ft 6in driving wheels the "Peacocks" were reliable engines, but they were eventually eclipsed by more powerful ones. Above the engine is the 1903 bridge over which parcels were wheeled. A survey in 1928 showed that 380 people worked at the station, well over half a million passengers a week used it, and over 750 trains arrived or departed. *(RK Blencowe)*

Inside the Train Shed, Platform 13. A subway from Great Ducie Street had been in place for some time before the creation of the two island platforms, and platform 6 was widened to allow vehicles to use this access. On it was built a large booking office with large clock faces. From here, most of the expresses were dealt with, although some York to Liverpool trains used platform 5 (later 11). Blowing off impatiently is 4-4-2 engine No 1393, one of the first of two groups of twenty built in 1899. Initially allocated to Newton Heath, it was later transferred to Leeds. It looks massive – the boiler was almost 9ft above rail level and it had 7ft 3in driving wheels, hence the nickname "High Flyers". The trailing wheels were originally sprung on the inside, but due to rough riding, they were replaced on the outside, as seen here. These engines, the pride and joy of the L&Y, worked their crack expresses to Liverpool, Southport, Blackpool and one turn to Windermere. Eastward destinations were York, Leeds and Bradford. There are numerous stories of their feats along the line to Liverpool when speeds of 100mph were allegedly attained. One of these fast trains ran to Liverpool every hour in 1910. *(BPC)*

Westbound Arrival, 1936. Having just passed East Junction signalbox, this train is about to enter platform 12. Increasing trainloads led to the development of more powerful engines, and in 1908 these 4-6-0 locos were built at the company's works at Horwich to the design of Mr Hughes. The locos did not live up to the performances expected of them, and they were very heavy on coal, earning them the

nickname "Dreadnoughts". At the end of 1919, the whole class was called into the works to sort out their problems. All but five were rebuilt with superheaters and Walschaerts valve gear, making them competent performers. Another 64 were built incorporating these alterations, and the example here is ex-L&Y No 1658 which became LMS No 10429, lasting until 1948. Note the cute ground signals. *(W Potter)*

Westbound Departure, Pre-Grouping. Setting out from platform 12 was a completely "foreign" experience. The engine is Midland Railway 4-4-0 No 384 and the coaches are from that company too – it is likely that the train is on its way to Scotland along MR lines, which will be gained at Hellifield. To get there, the train will pass via Bolton and Clitheroe. To the right is the pair of lines that the LNWR used to pass through Victoria station on its way east, the controlling signals being above the first coach. Of the two island platforms, this one (12 and13) was the widest. Midway along was the 2-storey booking office for passengers using the Great Ducie Street entrance. Accommodation for the Station Master was above, and opening in 1893, was a 10-lever signalbox that became disused before 1928. All this would have been under the roof of the train shed until World War II. *(CM & JM Bentley)*

Victoria East Junction, 1931. These two pictures were taken from the end of platform 11 looking east, and illustrate well the main line routes for trains to and from the east. Coming into the station past the 1889 signalbox with 108 levers is Aspinall class 5 2-4-2T No 10912. It is bringing empty stock from Red Bank carriage sidings that could form a train to Southport. The four lines curving away to the left formed the chief route east for L&Y trains. The magnificent signal gantry bristles with L&Y lower quadrant arms. In 1896, the layout was altered and L&Y interlocking replaced the original Railway Signal Co interlocking. Going via Cheetham Hill Junction, L&Y trains avoided the steep Miles Platting bank and congestion with the LNWR trains. This loop rejoined the main line at Thorpes Bridge Junction. *(BKB Green)*

Victoria East Junction, c1960. Steelwork for the new signal cabin has been erected on the left. Originally, the main lines were those to the right, rising up on the steep Miles Platting bank at 1 in 59 and stiffening to 1 in 47 within the first mile. These were quadrupled, but as they were used by both the L&Y and the LNWR, they still couldn't cope. As LNWR trains turned east

at Miles Platting Junction, 1½ miles away, the L&Y built a quadruple loop line from here in 1896 to avoid the incline and then rejoin the main line north of Miles Platting. The company then effectively abandoned the incline to the LNWR. This view is included as it shows a rare event – a calling on arm being off. Even though the track is occupied by the freight train in the distance, this engine, ex-L&Y 0-6-0 No 52271, can pass signals in the on position, as the smaller arm below indicates that this is permitted. Soon it will reach the train in front, and buffer up to the brake van. *(J Davenport)*

Overhead Parcels Carrier. By the late 1880s, the L&Y was handling around 860,000 parcels a year, often blocking the platforms. To solve the problem, Aspinall as CME, devised an overhead carrier consisting of a basket capable of carrying 15 cwt, and driven by a boy sitting above it. The basket was able to be lifted and lowered at each platform. A new parcels office was opened in December 1894 adjacent to platform 16 at the junction of New Bridge Street and Great Ducie Street. This unique device moved around a circular route over all the platforms, but good idea that it was, it wasn't trouble free. As late as 1919, coaches were still lit by gas, which sometimes required someone to climb onto their roofs to give them attention in the five minutes or so that some trains stopped here. On 26th February, the overhead carrier knocked a young woman from the roof of a coach at platform 14, and the injuries she sustained were fatal. The air raid on the night of 23rd/24th December 1940 destroyed the office and most of the roof over the western ends of the platforms, so putting an end to this machine, unique on the L&Y. *(BPC)*

Manchester Victoria, c1964. One can almost hear the puffing of the exhaust as it echoes from the adjacent wall of the old workhouse. Platform 17 was a short bay facing east, and setting out from there is a parcels train headed by class 5 4-6-0 No 45203. It was one of a batch of a hundred engines from Armstrong Whitworth, which at £5,119 each when built in 1935, was the lowest price for the entire class. It was to last until the end of steam on BR in 1968. *(G Coltas)*

Manchester Victoria, Train Indicator, c1922. This all-weather train indicator listed many, but not all, of the destinations of trains from the station. At the turn of the 20th century, there were around 600 passenger train arrivals and departures a day, 80 through freight trains, and additional specials, making Victoria by far the busiest of the L&Y stations – probably busier than any outside London. This type

of information board was commissioned by the L&Y after World War I. Excursions, especially on Bank Holidays, had always been a problem here. Special trains would run to Southport and Blackpool, as well as the Lake District, the company controlling passengers by issuing numbered tickets for specific trains. Another method of control was used in 1899 when the company ran out of rolling stock – they simply closed the booking office until sufficient coaches could be found. In the late 1920s there could be 140 Bank Holiday specials, 47 for Blackpool alone. When Queen Victoria opened the Manchester Ship Canal, 181,000 passengers used the station, illustrating the movement of people on a scale that we cannot imagine today, except in motorway traffic jams! *(BPC)*

Manchester Victoria, Circulating Area, 1955. This would be the scene for a passenger walking in through the Long Millgate entrance. They will have just passed the gentlemen's toilets and on the left are the booking office windows. To the right are the suburban platforms, complete with iron grills that can be drawn across to close the platform. In essence, not a lot has altered over the last 50 years – some trains still depart from these platforms. One big difference is that the trams that run from Bury to Altrincham pass through the area to the extreme right, then across the road and up the gradient to Piccadilly. On 10th

December 1947, a train of oil tanks ran away when trying to ascend the Miles Platting bank. The signalmen diverted it into platform 7, where it demolished the hydraulic buffers, and mounted the concourse seen here. While prompt action by the station staff prevented a fire from the leaking tanks, the unfortunate driver lost his life. *(Stations UK)*

Manchester Victoria, Exterior, 1880s. Hunts Bank refers to the eastern side of the River Irwell, the road becoming Great Ducie Street after it has passed north under the railway lines. Thus, the vehicular access to the station, Hunts Bank Approach, was an easterly road branching from its namesake. Looking up the approach, this view shows the original building on the left, its upper storey extending from the primary building. Inside were through lines and the single platform that the two companies shared. Expansion to the east brought a building at right angles to the original one, seen here at the end of the street, and opening in 1865. A

platform to the north opened then, with the island platforms a product of the 1880s developments. The station was rebuilt several times, but today's station is reminiscent of the arrangements of over 100 years ago.

Manchester Victoria, Exterior. Looking up Hunts Bank Approach we see the original building and its upper extension complete with clock on the extreme left. As part of the 1889 improvements, vehicular access to the station was altered to include a road, Victoria Station Approach, crossing of the River Irk, to the south of the station. This road joined up with the original Hunts Bank Approach at right angles, as can be seen here. The once white stone buildings date from a sweeping away of offices along Victoria Station Approach, and the completion of an office block along Todd Street and Station Approach in 1909, designed by William Dawes. Access to the station takes passengers past a map of the company's system originally painted red on white bricks. In 1979, the building was cleaned to reveal the original stone. *(BPC)*

Manchester Victoria, Exterior, 1960. For many years the footbridge from Corporation Street (and hence the Royal Exchange) across the River Irk was a source of complaint. A roadway was provided from 1900. The imposing office block went from Hunts Bank Approach along a straightened Victoria Station Approach to its junction with Long Mill Gate. There, a handsome curve was built with an entrance to the right into the suburban platforms. Along the straightened road was an awning that included many of the destinations that the L&Y ran to in stained glass, including for example, "The Continent". There was also a covered section across the road that allowed cabs to wait under cover to collect passengers. This was made ready for a visit of King Edward VII on 12th July 1905, but a single-decker bus ran into the support for the canopy in 1937, and brought about its demise. The bus was not too badly damaged. *(AC Gilbert)*

Acknowledgements

Like all books, this volume would not have seen the light of day if it hadn't been for the efforts of a large number of people, and the help of numerous organisations. The continual encouragement, support and advice of the team at Kestrel Railway Books has been invaluable. The efforts by many members of the Signalling Record Society enabled details to be corrected. Special mention must go to the Lancashire & Yorkshire Railway Society, whose helpfulness and willingness to offer technical data has made this book an enjoyable exercise. Mention must also go to the staff of the local history sections of the libraries at Liverpool, Kirkby, Wigan, Bolton, Salford and Manchester. The maps at the National Monuments Record Centre have proved to be an invaluable resource. Personal thanks go to Barry Lane, David Hampson and Graeme Earl for offering pictures from their collections. Many thanks also to Fred Collinge, Mike Fitton, Tom Wray, Paul Shackcloth, AC Gilbert and many others too. Thanks must go to WD Cooper for taking some really excellent pictures, and to his grandson David, for allowing them to see the light of day from across the Channel. Finally, thanks to John Horne for his help, and for allowing the use of his tickets.

All books like this have gaps in them, where (for one reason or another) no pictorial record seems to exist. My biggest gap must be of trains passing on the flyover at Brindle Heath – this would have been a magnificent sight. Others are the signalling works at Fazakerley, trains on the Wigan avoiding line and trains passing along the gradients to Salford Docks and Irwell Street goods yard. No doubt I will now be inundated with such rare pictures – such is life!

LIVERPOOL
&MANCHESTER by Bob Pixton

Look for the other titles in this Kestrel Railway Books series:

1: LNWR Lines. Lime Street to Exchange and London Road back to Lime Street.

2: Cheshire Lines. The route between Liverpool Central and Manchester Central.